MICHAEL BURGE is an Australian journalist and writer who was born at Inverell in the New England region of NSW. He grew up in the Blue Mountains, lived in England for most of the 1990s, and now resides on Coochiemudlo Island in Queensland's Moreton Bay with his husband and their two dogs.

TITLES BY MICHAEL BURGE

Fiction

Closet His, Closet Hers

Literary non-fiction

Merely Players: Acting like Shakespeare really matters

Non-fiction

Questionable Deeds: Making a stand for equal love

Pluck: Exploits of the single-minded

Write, Regardless! A no-nonsense guide to plotting, packaging & promoting your book

Plays

Merely Players

For information about upcoming titles go to
www.burgewords.com

MERELY PLAYERS

Omnibus edition

MICHAEL BURGE

*'All the world's a stage,
And all the men and women merely players.'*

William Shakespeare, *As You Like It*, Act 2, Scene VII

First published in Australia in 2016 by www.burgewords.com
Copyright © Michael Burge 2016

The moral right of the author has been asserted.

All rights reserved. No part of this book may be reproduced or transmitted by any person or entity in any form or by any means, electronic or mechanical, including photocopying, recording or by any information storage or retrieval system, without prior permission in writing from the author.

Applications for a performance license, whether amateur, educational or professional, must be made in writing with the publisher prior to the commencement of rehearsals.

National Library of Australia
Cataloguing-in-Publication data:

Burge, Michael, 1970-
Merely Players: Acting like Shakespeare really matters

ISBN: 9780994388711 (paperback)

Subjects: Actors--Drama.
Aging--Drama.
Comedy.

Dewey Number: A822.4

This is a work of literary non-fiction. Names, characters, businesses, places, events and incidents are either the products of the author's imagination or used in a fictitious manner. Some names and identifying details have been changed to protect the privacy of individuals.

Contents

Introduction
Merely Players – Acting like Shakespeare really matters 1
LGBTI Labour's Lost – A case for transgender players 137
Merely Players – A two-act play 143
Act One 147
Act Two 191
Shakespeare – A farmer who cultivated words 221
Acknowledgements

To everyone who ever stood before a crowd, head full of a writer's words, and pretended to be someone else

Introduction

THEATRE PEOPLE KNOW the art of making a play is very, very hard work. Real life is simply a matter of turning on the phone-cam, whereas the creation of a piece of drama or comedy is an ongoing process of questioning and exploring, usually starting with a script on the page.

This book is the story of my journey with one piece of work that took me thirteen years to manifest. *Merely Players* was an idea I had in my teens, revived as my youth was waning, and still haunts me in middle age. Of all the projects I ever started, it is one of the few I have refused to give up on, and it's the piece of literature that has been my greatest teacher in learning the writing process.

Along the way I've felt the bitter sting of rejection more times than I am willing to admit.

Unpublished and un-produced work is easily delivered to the bottom drawer of any writer's desk, but sometimes it's not easy to leave it there. This is probably a mixture of ego and bloody-mindedness, bad luck and the shortcomings of the work itself; however, when a writer knows a good story, a certain amount of persistence is required if the marketplace is slow to recognise it.

The most recent example of this process was the two-decade development of Phyllis Nagy's screenplay adaptation of Patricia Highsmith's novel *Carol*, which languished in what writer's call 'development hell' until the right production team came along.

In interviews, Nagy admitted how match-fit the long

wait made her, able to adjust her work quickly and subtly to match the visions of new stakeholders; yet she also admitted the years showed her the value of her original work when new production teams inspired her to put old ideas back in that had been discarded by temporary collaborators along the way.

Merely Players has been a bit like that for me, but it has also been a companion.

The focus required to commit to a full-length work kept me going through some very dark times, so much that the play has come to symbolise a lot about me as a person, my thoughts and feelings about ageing, sexual and gender diversity, and the politics of storytelling in the modern theatre.

After the latest rejection of my work, I retreated into writing in order to bring *Merely Players* to life for readers, not really knowing if the result fitted into any genre. Adapting a play into a piece of literary non-fiction requires the writer to direct the play's action, in a sense, which has made what might have been a labour into a delight.

I also broke a cardinal rule about authorship that was around at the dawn of my writing career, about not putting yourself in the story, yet finding there was more of the tale to tell by opening the gate on my role.

I hope the finished product gives insights into the writing process, showing that life for actors and writers has not really changed much in the four hundred years since William Shakespeare was creating plays for his company of actors, The King's Men.

When Shakespeare died in April 1616, he left several problems for his colleagues. The years between his death and the publication of what became known as The First Folio of his collected plays in 1623, a process spearheaded by Shakespeare's fellow actors John Heminges and Henry Condell, were a litany of loss and harried industry that only seemed to accelerate in the wake of lead actor Richard Burbage's death in 1619.

Historians have speculated about exactly how the publication was paid for, edited and printed. The theories include Germaine Greer's quite valid assertion in her well-argued study *Shakespeare's Wife* (Bloomsbury, 2007) that the project could have been spearheaded and funded by Ann Shakespeare (née Hathaway).

Despite Greer's well-documented blindspot for realities about transgender women, her work on bringing to life the under-documented life of Ann Hathaway sheds more light on the Shakespearean canon than it has ever been given genuine credit for, and was a great source of inspiration for me when using similar techniques to flesh out the transgender protagonist of *Merely Players* – Mistress Wilkinson, alias Nicholas Tooley.

As is typical with Shakespeare, there are plenty of clues but not much hard evidence.

The best explanation of the publication of the Folio I ever found was that written by actor and teacher Doug Moston in the introduction to his facsimile edition of *The First Folio of Shakespeare 1623* (Applause Theatre & Cinema Book Publishers, New York, 1995).

Moston's exploration of the Folio, from its typography to its many clues and cues for actors, recreates the performance conditions of the original Shakespearean players. It reveals much about how attitudes to rehearsals and script management have changed over time.

No matter what any historian thinks of the plausibility of *Merely Players*, it would be hard to argue that the deaths of two company mainstays made things easy for The King's Men. The evidence that the First

Folio is full of errors and not the definitive versions of many of Shakespeare's plays (despite Heminges' and Condell's claim that it was) tells me there was a certain amount of desperation and pretence in its publication process.

It could also be argued it was one of the world's most important and best-selling independently-published books, and therefore inspiration for self-publishers everywhere.

Having worked as an actor, knowing the passion and drive it takes to perform, and also keenly aware of how the same ingredients go into writing, I am qualified to speak on these actors' behalf and imagine that they had the ability to rise above their station (players were considered by most to be little more than scum) and were far more influential than Shakespeare in delivering that which his work gave to the world. Without these players, 'The Bard' simply would not be.

But I already know what a great story it is...

Michael Burge, March 2016

Merely Players

Acting like Shakespeare really matters

All the world's a stage,
And all the men and women **merely players**;
They have their exits and their entrances,
And one man in his time plays many parts,
His acts being seven ages. **At first, the infant**,
Mewling and puking in the nurse's arms.
Then **the whining schoolboy**, with his satchel
And shining morning face, creeping like snail
Unwillingly to school. And then the lover,
Sighing like furnace, with a woeful ballad
Made to his mistress' eyebrow. Then a soldier,
Full of strange oaths and bearded like the pard,
Jealous in honor, sudden and quick in quarrel,
Seeking the bubble reputation
Even in the cannon's mouth. And then the justice,
In fair round belly with good capon lined,
With eyes severe and beard of formal cut,
Full of **wise saws and modern instances**;
And so he plays his part. The sixth age shifts
Into the lean and slippered pantaloon,
With spectacles on nose and pouch on side;
His youthful hose, well saved, a world too wide
For his shrunk shank, and his big manly voice,
Turning again toward childish treble, pipes
And whistles in his sound. Last scene of all,
That ends **this strange eventful history**,
Is second childishness and mere oblivion,
Sans teeth, sans eyes, sans taste,
sans everything.

William Shakespeare, As You Like It, Act 2, Scene VII

At first, the infant

A SKIRT HAS not much more cloth to it than a cloak, and it was my cloak that was my first skirt. My friend Ada, the daughter of the kitchen maid in my Grandpapa's house, showed me how to wear it, and together we fashioned a way to have it hang from my smock, tied with an apron at the back.

Although we laughed about it when I stood on the kitchen table and danced up and down, Ada's mama told me to take it off before I went in to see mine.

But today, I forgot about it, and Mama looks at me over her needlework, her eyes wide, as my horrid future dances across her face. Even as the corners of her mouth begin to lift, I know it is not with mirth, but anger.

She calls me to her by slapping the silk of her skirt, just as she calls her little dogs, and when I am slow to move, she tears at the apron. As my cloak comes away she whips my legs with her flat hand and sends me to my bed.

I do not sleep, because last time she caught me playing with Ada in the alley, my cloak around my legs, she told me I would be sent to London, where my dead Papa once lived, and they'd call me an orphan.

Mama said Good Queen Bess would be my new mama after that, and they'd find me another home and I would never see her again.

She said all the men would notice a boy in a skirt, but I already knew they did not see I was a boy. Long before Mama discovered me, Ada and I had passed for a pair of girls from the big house, sisters perchance.

MERELY PLAYERS

IT is 1975 and I am under the coloured car rug in the back of my parents' Holden while Mum leans out the window buying tickets to a session of *Murder on the Orient Express* at the drive-in in the country town where I was born.

We're hiding because this is not a session for children. Why Mum has not left us at home with Dad at the farmhouse is a mystery to me at that age. I'm far more fascinated with my first experience of drive-in culture, particularly the fast food and the shark's tooth pendants for sale at the stand where the giant beast in the *Jaws* movie poster rises above the cafeteria.

Finishing off my chips and hot dog, my eyes become heavy at the end of the dream-like opening montage of Agatha Christie's murder mystery. The whine of strings heightens my senses, but the food in my belly, the late hour, and the comfort of being nestled in the seat against Mum sends me off to sleep before the story develops.

Later, I wake with a start, not due to a particularly loud scene up on the big screen, but because it has gone uncharacteristically quiet.

Against a high-pitched, menacingly subtle soundtrack, figures, in the half-darkness, are focussed on a terrible, stabbing task.

An array of 1970s movie stars, their demeanour so exaggerated they are like clowns to my unopened mind. Silent, deadly, determined. It is a powerful dose of dramatic tension for a farmer's son, and it plants a desire in me to be part of whatever magic went into its creation.

The whining schoolboy

IT IS 1984 and I am in my English class, the first room in the cold weatherboard block at the high end of a school in the Blue Mountains.

The class sits in pairs to read a play. As copies are handed around, the teacher explains it is time for us to start reading Shakespeare. We begin with *Macbeth*.

Some of the more popular, well-connected boys closer to the front of the class get to read the parts of Macbeth, Banquo and King Duncan.

I don't mind. The idea of performing in front of people has sent me into a panic ever since primary school, when the librarian cast me as a scolding caricature of a female schoolteacher in the class play and encouraged me to camp it up. No-one but her found the sight of me, dressed in one of my mother's wrap-around skirts, in the least bit funny.

One of the girls on the other side of the class reads Lady Macbeth, and there are sniggers when she says:

> *'Come, you spirits*
> *That tend on mortal thoughts, unsex me here,*
> *And fill me from the crown to the toe top-full*
> *Of direst cruelty.'*

Some of the boys allow their schoolyard conflicts to enter the play, reading their lines but adding comments under their breath where Shakespeare has not given them enough verbal power.

The murder is done. Lady Macbeth says:

> *'Retire we to our chamber.*
> *A little water clears us of this deed.*
> *How easy is it, then!'*

The English teacher stops and poses a question: 'Why

is it, can anyone tell me, that Shakespeare has written such a long, comic scene after the murders?'

I look at the book in my hand, clues eluding me. Nothing, apart from the Porter making jokes:

'Knock, knock, knock! Who's there, i' th' name of Beelzebub?
Here's a farmer that hanged himself on the expectation of plenty.'

'Think about it, everyone,' the teacher says, casting her knowing face across every one of her pupils. 'Macbeth and his wife have just killed King Duncan and his servants. They are holding knives, dripping with blood. Shakespeare has given the actors an entire scene *to clean themselves up.*'

In a rush it comes to me that these are not just words on a page, but scenes. Like old clothes, they lie waiting to be worn by others. With a well-rehearsed cut and fall in their very fabric, they can never go wrong.

It is probably the first adult thought I ever have about literature.

Sometime in the next few months, but well before the end of the year, I will realise I am gay.

In this new community, where me, my siblings and our mother escaped the country-town fallout after my parents' divorce, this frightening self discovery will require me to develop a sophisticated and long-term act.

I FIRST met Will when Master Burbage and I played *Romeo and Juliet*. I was the same age as a schoolboy, but I was never at school for long before Mama gave me to the playhouse.

Master Burbage has called me to run his lines, but Will wants to argue about the play.

ACTING LIKE SHAKESPEARE REALLY MATTERS

Master Burbage says the crowd will never cry for the lovers if they are laughing too much on the way to their tears, but Will tries to make Master Burbage see that it doesn't matter how hard he makes them laugh, they will always cry in the end.

Master Burbage tells Will to get out so we can run our lines.

'Just do it as written,' Will says, before he leaves.

I sit at my Master Burbage's feet and he drums his fingers on the table as we chatter through his lines like a pair of birds. He is word-perfect.

After he tells me to retire to my place under the stage to run my own lines, he says I will make a pretty lass as Juliet; but when he says it, he doesn't look at me.

But Will was in the right. They laughed at us in *Romeo and Juliet*, and then they cried, and then they cheered.

One man in his time

IT IS 1989 and I am a total geek. I'm a year-and-a-half out of school and somehow I have segued from academia across to vocational training in the theatre. I'm sitting in a rehearsal room at Australia's pre-eminent drama school, the National Institute of Dramatic Art (NIDA).

The fabulously dressed, wildly attractive student body kindly stops at my flopping fringe and asks me no searching questions, although I always sense them hanging in the air.

Once a week, we design students enter these mysterious upstairs rehearsal spaces, with their lilac-coloured vinyl chairs and puce hessian walls, for a quick whiz through the great traditions of the profession we're all on the cusp of.

Flying through a session on Elizabethan theatre, we slow down briefly at Shakespeare and the Globe playhouse. Our lecturer underlines this as the hotbed that gave rise to the Shakespearean canon – thirty-seven full-length plays, many of which became staples of Western theatre.

He makes a throwaway comment, in a manner suggesting we should already know, that after Shakespeare's death in 1616, a group of his acting colleagues published his plays in the one book – known as the First Folio – and had they not done so, around half of these plays, including perennial crowd pleasers *Twelfth Night* and *Macbeth*, would be completely lost to us today, since they were not recorded or published anywhere else.

While the lecturer moves on to the Restoration, theatre's bawdy return to form after the puritanical years

ACTING LIKE SHAKESPEARE REALLY MATTERS

of Civil War, I flip open our large required text to find the reference. There is little detail, but it credits players John Heminges and Henry Condell with overseeing the publication of one large book of Shakespeare's plays in 1623.

I fill in the gaps by daydreaming, where I have no barriers to imagining what this action looked like.

I see a church, Shakespeare's body being laid in the floor, and his acting colleagues mourning the loss of their mainstay. Shafts of light fall on old players, gathering to remember. Among them, perhaps, are the actors who first played *Romeo and Juliet*.

Which of them gets the idea? Who decides what they must do in order to preserve this writer's body of work?

Surely, I think, my evocative, Baroque picture brings one of the miracles of the modern theatre into the light. Long before I make myself visible enough to inhabit a scene, capable of exploring this act of preservation with more than just images, it settles into my heart.

Yet right at the idea's conception, I somehow miss a very important detail: everyone else in that rehearsal room acts as though it's unremarkable that half the plays of Shakespeare had almost been completely lost.

GOOD Queen Bess has been in her grave sixteen years when I return, and I am seven-and-thirty years of age. Nobody stops me when I pass through the tiring house, from which I glimpse the wall of faces on three levels, closing on us like a jeering enemy that has breached the battlements and is marauding its way down the inside of a dark tower.

The expectant flesh of the crowd hangs in the light from the hole of blue sky above, shouting crudely for the men on the stage, as though it might wash across the narrow divide and seek out every burrow a player could hide in.

Before I am forced to look one of these thousand monkeys in the eye, I escape down the rough-edged hole in the floor, large enough for a man to fall through if he did not take care.

As my eyes adjust to the darkness, I let my toes find the edge of each step. They are not level and curve around in a manner which means even I, as short as I am, must tuck my head into my shoulders to pass without hitting it.

Light streams through the cracks above and dust falls with it, throwing glowing strips along a mess of costumes on which a thousand specks collect. It's as though clouds of gold have come to rest on the shoulders of once-great men, now invisible.

The players on the stage above walk up and down for their calls, making the beams groan. This sends more gold down upon me as I reach the floor and smell the worn soil. Only then do I know I am back in the playhouse.

There is a patch of light for my basket, and nearby a box I can use as a stool. I unwrap my sliver of mirror from its coloured rag and see my eye flash past, then my cheek.

It will not do, so, holding my face half in the golden light, and half in the welcoming darkness, I fuss with my paints as another call goes up from the crowd.

'God gave you a face, but you make yourself a better one,' I see my lips saying. 'Is that right?' I ask, out loud. 'God gave you your face, and yet you make yourself another...' I say, trying again.

But it is not right. I tut, hold the mirror at arm's

length to take in my whole visage, and say: 'Mistress Wilkinson, you have forgotten your lines!'.

Something about my own wan face looking back at me draws the forgotten words back into me.

'God gave you one face, and you make yourself another!'

I relish it. 'That's right. That's word-perfect,' I say, and I am calm again.

The crowd unleashes another burst of applause, so I take it, even though when I stand and curtsy I feel the pain in my knees. I bend my chin to my chest at the last moment, in the becoming way.

For a moment, all the cheering is for me.

Then, noise on the stairs above. The sound of men falling over themselves.

I recognise Master Burbage first. His gait is slower, but I can see he is the same man, as he turns at the foot of the stairs, shoves his brightly coloured cape into my arms, pushes aside a rude curtain and starts pulling at the strings of his hose in order to piss in a pot.

'Sweet relief... get the barrel open, lads,' he says to the one with the white clown face, who dumps his hat on my head.

'Aye, but hurry it up in there Burbage,' white-face says. It is Master Condell, still playing the Fool.

'Just wait your turn Condell, I might get another call,' Master Burbage says, turning so that I can see the glistening stream that comes out of him as he misfires.

'There's no calls yet,' the third man says. He carries himself more upright than the others, although the light, or the dust, is making him blink. It is Master Heminges, without a doubt, but his face is so lined it casts shadows across itself.

'Oh, they'll call for me Heminges, just wait for it,' Master Burbage says.

MERELY PLAYERS

None of them knows me yet, so I start to put away their costumes, as the crowd begins to stamp its feet; yet it feels like silence down here, with three boisterous old men making not one sound, straining to hear if any calls will come.

Master Burbage squeezes the last of his piss out, but he does not come out from the privy. He is looking for something.

'If you two buggers are going to keep pissing in my pot, be sure to replace the privy paper when you've used it all!' he says, fetching a handful of papers from his things and handing it to Heminges, who rushes into the privy.

'Good of you, Burbage, to allow us a share of the room,' Heminges says.

'My private dressing room,' Master Burbage growls from his chair.

'Private doss-house, more like,' Condell says, trying to get a barrel to start flowing.

'Can it, clown,' Master Burbage says.

Condell is pushing and pulling at the spigot, and it's making a sound that nobody likes when the call comes, distant at first, but unmistakeable.

Bur-bage, Bur-bage, Bur-bage!

'They're calling for me, but I cannot go after playing so small a part,' Master Burbage says, motionless, turned away from the light.

'It might have been a small part, but the crowd loved you, you must go!' Condell says, his white face lit by a crack above his head.

'Only if you think I should,' Master Burbage mutters, starting to turn.

'We'll follow you, go on!' Heminges says, pulling up his codpiece.

ACTING LIKE SHAKESPEARE REALLY MATTERS

'Wait for me, I'm about to burst!' Condell says, wanting his turn at the pot.

Bur-bage, Bur-bage, Bur-bage!

'Burbage cannot wait, they're calling him!' Heminges says.

'I'll leave it then, we'll go... go!' Condell says, standing at the other side of the stairs, making a gateway for Burbage.

For a moment, I think he will not go. From where I stand, making room on a crooked costume rail for the things Heminges dropped at my feet, I see a very old man, tapping one hand on the bench in front of him, and gripping his other hand in a fist.

Then he is gone, past the other men in a flourish. At the last moment I see a glimpse of his face, rising into the light, coming to life. The boards above my head groan with the weight of three more men, and the crowd ignites for Master Burbage.

Bur-bage, Bur-bage, Bur-bage!

I could do with the privy myself. Accustomed to taking my chance whenever it comes, I gather my skirts and back my way in, trying not to touch the rank curtain, but it is too narrow.

I stop, then, gathering my skirts higher until I hold them away from my legs, I reach for my cock and piss standing up.

By the time the men return, I'm back at the costume rail, patting the front of my skirts down, hanging things up from the pile in the centre of the room that appears to have been mounting up for years.

Condell makes the right turn at the foot of the stairs, his cock already out as he just makes it to mix his piss with ours.

'No more, I can do no more. Pour me a drink,'

Master Burbage says, sitting.

'I need to be empty before I take any more on board!' Condell calls from the privy.

So I collect the cups from their place on Condell's bench, and pour every man a drink. Master Burbage snatches his and downs it in one.

Bur-bage, Bur-bage, Bur-bage!

'I couldn't possibly manage another climb,' he says, snorting drink down his front.

'Of course you could,' Heminges says.

'What about the men who played the leads, what would they think of me, hogging all the calls?' Master Burbage asks, his eyes glinting.

'They're not calling for the other men, they're calling for the great Richard Burbage. That's why they come to the Globe playhouse, to see Richard Burbage, the shining light of The King's Men, England's finest company of players. Get up there!' Heminges says.

Bur-bage, Bur-bage, Bur-bage!

'Another drink,' Master Burbage demands, wagging his cup.

I fill it quickly. The old man throws it down with a gasp and heaves himself upright.

'When I get up top, leave me, I can manage from there,' he says, lunging at the stairs. I see his face in the light again, but it is not coming to life. The other men follow him, trying to help.

The boards groan and I get another round of drinks ready. Heminges and Condell return first, but their energy has faded.

Bur-bage, Bur-bage, Bur-bage!

'Shouldn't we wait up top and help him down?' Condell asks, pacing at the bottom of the steps.

'He's better at getting down by himself,' Heminges

ACTING LIKE SHAKESPEARE REALLY MATTERS

replies, rubbing gold dust from his eyes.

'Nay, when the crowd's calling, it takes twenty years off him.'

'Watch for him, and help if he needs it.'

'Aye, but I need a drink,' Condell says.

I pour them one each, just as Master Burbage shouts from the top of the steps.

'Heminges, Condell, come, assist!'

The other men throw their necks back to drink, then go to assist.

'It's only that I hurt my knees, doing all that kneeling in the play,' Master Burbage whines, until the other men retrieve him from the corner of the stairwell.

'You need to sit down before the next play. Woman, a drink for Master Burbage,' Heminges says, as he and Condell lower Master Burbage into his chair.

I bring them all a fresh drink.

'Cheers!' Master Burbage manages.

'Cheers,' Heminges responds, puffing from the effort.

'To our next play,' Condell says, rubbing his right knee as he sits.

'What are we doing?' Master Burbage utters into the silence.

Only it's not real silence, just a crowd silence, of people buying pies and ale upstairs.

'You're playing *Romeo and Juliet*,' I say.

Up until now, none of them has looked, but now their old eyes fall on me, standing in the shadow of the rack I have filled with crushed costumes from the floor.

Heminges almost laughs: 'The washer woman knows what play we're doing, but we players do not?' he says.

'Heminges, hold off, we haven't had a whore call on us in ages!' Condell replies.

'Come to think of it, we haven't had a washer woman

see to us in ages,' Heminges says.

Master Burbage raises a finger: 'Never speak of the washer women as whores!'

Then I speak.

'Master Condell, there isn't gold enough in your pocket for the likes of me.'

'I've gold enough, for a pretty lass. Come into the light. Let me see if you're worth it,' Condell says, squinting.

I stay where I am, just behind the costumes, then, in a manner which commands their complete attention, I make my entrance, ensuring one of those strips of light falls across my face.

> *'What's here? A cup, closed in my true love's hand?*
> *Poison, I see, hath been his timeless end.*
> *Oh churl! drunk all, and left no friendly drop*
> *To help me after? I will kiss thy lips.'*

As I say it, I make my way towards Condell, whose laughter I stifle by taking his cup, downing his drink, and with one hand on his heavy jowls, I deliver a kiss to his trembling lips.

'She reminds me of my own Juliet,' Master Burbage says.

'A pretty scene, wench, but no woman plays on the stage. They would close us down for harbouring harlots!' Condell says, trying to hold me.

'I'm no washer woman, or a harlot, masters. We have all met before,' I say.

'I know the voice, but the face... can it be? Is it Nick Tooley?' Master Burbage says.

'Master Tooley?' Condell asks, wiping away my kiss. 'I would never have known you.'

'I haven't gone by that name for a very long time,' I say, smoothing down the front of my skirts again

ACTING LIKE SHAKESPEARE REALLY MATTERS

Heminges makes a dismissive sound. 'We haven't seen you at the playhouse these... ten years.'

'Oh, they stopped writing parts for old women long ago,' I say.

'Ah, we must be playing *Antony and Cleopatra*, but your costume's not too queenly,' Heminges says, mocking.

I shake my head. 'Nay, I only came to visit Master Burbage, and it's *Romeo and Juliet*, I'm sure of it.'

Master Burbage heaves himself upright and spreads his arms wide. 'What do you think of our new digs? Rougher than upstairs, but less crowded.'

'Aye, it is a little different to the old days,' I say, remembering it was the boy players who attired ourselves down here, not old men.

'Come, Tooley, they won't have got you back for Juliet. Cleopatra's more your thing,' Heminges says, unbuttoning his doublet.

'Nobody "got me back", Master Heminges, and I read the playbill when I came in. It announces *Romeo and Juliet* as the afternoon play, clear as day.'

Heminges does not meet my eye. 'If it's Juliet, you'll be needing a veil or two,' he says, snorting to hold in his laughter, which sets off Condell.

'Master Burbage, do you know what is being played this afternoon?' I ask.

'They never bring us a playbill down here. Someone will have to fetch it,' Master Burbage says.

But the other men remain seated, busying themselves with loosening clothing and downing their drinks.

I speak into the silence. 'Since it seems I have lost my memory, I'd better go.'

MERELY PLAYERS

IT is 1990 and I am sitting next to my mother in one of the rehearsal rooms at NIDA. She's come down from the Blue Mountains to see a student production with me, but she's looking fragile.

A few months prior, she had exploratory surgery. They found her abdomen and several major organs in the grip of cancer, removed a kidney, ovaries and a section of bowel, closed her up again and sent her home.

She's not letting on about her plan to avoid chemotherapy as long as possible. No-one wants to talk about death at a dream factory like a drama school.

The acting students in my year are performing a matinee of *Pericles, Prince of Tyre*. My flatmate is in the cast, playing Thaisa, Pericles' wife.

In the penultimate scene, when wife, husband and daughter are reunited, I sense my mother looking intently at the action, made golden by the spotlights hitting the honey-coloured parquetry floor, the light reflecting into the faces of the cast.

The characters rediscover one another across that triangle of light, and it's not so much the language but the moment that touches my mother. A family is restored after all were feared not only estranged, but dead. Pericles says:

'O, come, be buried
A second time within these arms.'

It plants a seed of faith in Mum. Afterwards, she insists I tell my flatmate how much seeing this play has helped. I am too scared to ask how.

I CAN hear them arguing downstairs. Just above the turn in the steps, I wait, and I listen.

'You might have poured Tooley a jar,' Master

Burbage says, and I see his shadow stalking between them.

'Master Tooley never liked to carouse with the men, as I recall,' Heminges says.

'Then leave off the arguing, give him a chance to see if he likes it again,' Master Burbage says.

'I thought he went to his grave, long ago. What's he doing back here?' Heminges asks.

'He is one of our very finest players.'

'Did you ask him back?' Heminges demands.

'We've got to have our best players, if we're to fill a season,' Master Burbage replies.

'We'd all better be word-perfect, or Master Tooley – the playhouse pedant – will be on every man's back about getting his words right,' Heminges says.

'Master Tooley is a long-standing member of this company, make him welcome,' Master Burbage shouts.

'How long since he played on the stage?' Heminges asks.

'Any one of our players can come and go as he pleases,' Master Burbage says.

'Will he be attired in women's weeds as he comes and goes?'

'Why? Are you thinking of lifting his skirt?' Master Burbage asks, laughing.

'We're none of us sodomites down here!' Heminges says, incredulous.

'Nay,' Master Burbage says. 'Now, Heminges, you must pick up the pace at the end. You left me waiting again.'

'I will,' he says, clearly, then mutters, 'and try not to damage my hearing...'

'What was that?' Master Burbage spits.

'Nothing,' Heminges replies quickly, 'I was just

reminding Condell not to tread on all my lines.'

'That's right,' Master Burbage says, 'Condell, one laugh is good, two is great, but three is...'

'Greedy, I know. I can't help it,' Condell says, taking the reprimand in a gale of laughter. 'Once I get them giggling up the back, it comes washing over me like a wave and sets me off again.'

'Like a cheap clown, you went after every other man's laughs,' Master Burbage says.

I take that as my cue and start down the stairs, where I find Heminges and Condell sitting, like overgrown schoolboys.

'Do we have the play yet? Tooley, go and ask what we're playing,' Master Burbage says.

'You already sent him,' Condell says.

Master Burbage blinks. 'I did?'

'Take it slow on the slop, old man,' Condell says.

'I could drink you under the table, both of you,' Master Burbage growls, reaching for his cup. 'Ah, Tooley. What have we got?'

I read from the playbill: '"The tragedy of *Romeo and Juliet*, featuring the great Richard Burbage and other players of The King's Men, at the Globe playhouse in the afternoon, with entertainments before and after",' before casting it down on Heminges' table and crossing to the costume rack.

Heminges says, quietly: 'I see you have not lost your perfect memory, Master Tooley.'

'And you still have a liking for ordering every man about, Master Heminges,' I reply.

Master Burbage pushes his chair back and stretches. 'I shall have to say no to playing Romeo today. A message must be sent to young Joseph Taylor to come to the playhouse in an urgent fashion to go on for me, he's been drilled in the part.'

'Master Taylor is already in the playhouse, Burbage,' Heminges says.

'I thought they'd hired him out,' Master Burbage says. 'Did you see him?' he asks me.

'Aye,' I lie.

'How's he looking, leggy?'

'I didn't see his legs.'

'They'll have young Nathan Field in for Juliet, since Master Tooley's not up to it,' Heminges says, scratching at the back of his neck.

'Nonsense. Tooley and I could play the lovers, even now,' Master Burbage says, settling in. 'In our day they could call any play, any play by William Shakespeare at least, and we'd be ready after just donning our robes. Romeo, Othello, Lear... and Tooley as Juliet, Desdemona and Cordelia... any one of them. Young, leggy players don't have the goods these days.'

'I'm only too happy to get to the alehouse early after whatever little bit they give me,' Condell mutters from his corner.

'Get yourselves up there and see what you're playing today. Tell them Master Tooley is available for Juliet,' Master Burbage commands.

'You need not tell them that,' I say.

'Nonsense, it's your role. If they want to put another man on in your place, they must ask you first. Heminges, you can tell Master Taylor he had better come see me if he wants to play Romeo... and bring us some leftover pies.'

Condell is on his feet at that. 'Now there's a good idea.'

'Condell, you go to the bakery and I'll see about the parts,' Heminges says as they hit the stairs.

I wait until I can hear the men talking in their careless manner upstairs, while I watch Master Burbage, who has kept his eyes closed since he leaned back in his chair.

The old man is still, apart from twitching his nose now and again, sniffing back the dust. He brushes a cobweb from his face. Perchance he thinks he is alone, because he starts when I speak.

'Are you well, Master Burbage, after the first play?'

'Very hale. Ready for another, always ready.'

'You didn't tell them I was coming,' I say. 'You didn't warn them about my manner, nowadays.'

'Aye, well, it's one thing to read of it in a letter, but it's another thing to see it before you. You might be in women's weeds, but you're still one of us, aren't you?' he asks, heaving himself upright.

'Let's just see how it goes,' I say.

But Master Burbage seems to be looking for something. When he doesn't find it on his table, he searches for it in his head. Then, looking into the darkness, he speaks.

'They laugh when it's a comedy, and they cry when it's a tragedy...'

I misunderstand. 'Aye, they do, but they still love Richard Burbage.'

'Not all love Burbage as much as they used,' he says, taking the thread. 'You've returned to us at a desperate time. Richard Burbage, the shining light of the Globe playhouse, is having to fight for good roles, and decent players like Heminges and Condell just get the slops.'

'There's plenty of good parts in *Romeo and Juliet*, if they don't give you Romeo.'

'My guess is they'll want me for the Apothecary. If so, they can find someone else.'

'But that is one of the most important roles. Without

the Apothecary, the story would not go the same way at the end.'

'He's just an afterthought Will Shakespeare put in to make his play work,' he says, full of regrets.

'Nay, he's a Potion Maker of Mantua. We must array you, come.'

I use the excuse of retrieving one of Master Burbage's cloaks from the back of his chair to get close to him.

The old man is leaning forward, so it only takes a swift motion to lift it up and away, but there is an odd sound to the fabric, coming from within. I lift it and immediately see the pages pinned inside. Play pages, fastened carelessly. Not written by hand, but printed letters.

Master Burbage has already risen and is lifting his chin. This is our old dance, so I must help him nudge his shoulders into the yolk of the cape and spread the fabric evenly around.

'Mrs Burbage will be pleased, very pleased, that you're back,' he mutters. 'Did I tell you we have another child this winter? That makes... ten, I think.'

I fuss with the fall of the cloak. 'Another *grand*child, surely, Master Burbage?'

But I am not prepared for his sudden anger. 'Do you know my children better than I?' he shouts.

I retreat a little, but continue to pull at the edges of his cloak, my eyes on the floor. 'Nay, Master Burbage.'

He inhales and lifts his shoulders, then forgives me: 'Mrs Burbage is always better pleased about me being in the playhouse all hours when she knows you are here to see after me.'

'Show me how it falls,' I say. He turns left and right. 'You look very fine,' I add.

'Nick?' he asks.

'Dickie?' I reply.

'You'll always be here, won't you, when I come off the stage?' he asks, eyes down.

'Aye, I will.'

He opens his arms to me and the cloak goes out to make the invitation. I accept. We kiss. His hands falter along my sides, around my long untouched waist, until the sounds of the others approaching down the steps sees us swiftly come apart.

Heminges and Condell are arguing as they return, and I am relieved, because that means they will not notice my hot face.

'I could add a jig. This fellow could be a musician, always playing a lute for his mistress,' Condell says. 'Where is my old lute?'

'Just stick to the role Condell,' Heminges commands, following.

'A Fool can always tell a joke or two, and nobody is going to stop him, it's not like I'm on a third-rate part,' Condell says, searching the mess of props by his table.

Heminges stops to make his point, like a boy. 'My part is second-rate, and no less. Montague is one of the Lords.'

Condell laughs into his belly. 'You are playing a mere storytelling device.'

But Heminges insists: 'There is Lord Capulet, Juliet's father, and then there is Lord Montague, Romeo's father, who is every bit as important as Lord Capulet.'

'Bollocks,' says Condell, straining to reach something.

'Condell thinks he's going to add bits here and there to fluff up his part,' Heminges says, noting the distance between me and Master Burbage.

'You'd do well to fluff up your own part and leave

mine well alone,' Condell adds, dragging his lute into the light.

Master Burbage brings things to an end: 'Cease your prattling and ready yourselves. Where are those young bucks, come to ask our permission to play the lovers?'

'Master Tooley is on near the start,' Heminges says, producing a woman's hat and veil for me. 'They sent these down for you. They needed someone for old Montague's wife, and I said you'd be perfect.'

'Hard luck, but think of it as a way to ease yourself back into playing,' Master Burbage says.

'I did not come back to play,' I say, putting the hat on the rack with some others.

'Then while you're on the stage, duckie, perchance you work out what it is you did come back for,' Heminges says, before turning to Master Burbage. 'You're the Apothecary, who gives Romeo the poison.'

'I know what the infernal Apothecary does!' Master Burbage shouts, pushing the back of his chair into Heminges.

'Condell is playing Peter, the servant to the nurse,' Heminges explains, retreating.

'A servant to a servant!' Condell jokes. 'They must cease this habit of giving me all the important roles.'

'It's royal robes this afternoon men, not togas. Put your helmets away and find yourself a feathered hat,' Heminges says. 'I'm Lord Montague, so I'll be in some of the big scenes,' he adds, sifting through the headwear.

I have been watching Heminges' swagger, and I go straight to cut him down. 'One scene, in truth, and if my pedant's brain serves me, you'll also have a little bit towards the middle.'

Heminges stops, raises his eyebrows. 'Ah, we can rely on you to remind us of our entrances and exits.'

'Nay, you cannot call on me when you drop your lines, Master Heminges,' I say. 'I'll take my leave and give my role to one of the boys upstairs.'

'Tell one of them he's playing the Apothecary. Burbage will not,' Master Burbage announces, then sniffs.

But Heminges is having none of it. 'I'm sure there'll be spare boys willing to go on for you two, only find one that looks and sounds like the great Richard Burbage, because the crowd is expecting to see him. It said so, duckie, on your little piece of paper.'

We fall silent, which increases the volume of the expectant crowd, returning from the yard.

I turn to Master Burbage: 'Will you stay and play the Apothecary, if I go on with you?'

'Nay... I'll go on for a bigger role, but not that one,' he replies, fiddling with his thumbs.

'You and I are on as soon as they sound the trumpets. Array yourself!' Heminges tells me.

I go back to the place I have made for myself by the rack. Master Burbage sulks while the others begin to peel doublets over expanded bellies, revealing sweaty waists and backs. I notice Heminges undoing his hose on the other side of the rack, trying to conceal himself.

'Masters, I have seen a man out of his clothes before, and not tried to make him mine, but if you'd be more comfortable hiding your glorious forms, I can wait upstairs,' I say.

'Nay, your place is down here with us. We're not going to make a fuss about Master Tooley, now are we?' Heminges asks.

Condell shakes his head.

'Perchance you just sit by the steps and tell me if you can spot any printer's boys in the crowd,' Heminges adds, pointing to the ceiling.

'You're letting printers into the playhouse now?' I ask, crossing to the stairs.

'Much has changed since you were in the playhouse, Master Tooley. They'll have real women playing soon enough,' Condell says.

'Don't believe him, it will never happen,' Master Burbage mutters into his lap.

'And there's never a rehearsal for the bit players, because there's no lines apart from whatever you can drag up from within your receptacle,' Condell adds, tapping the side of his head.

I search the ceiling by the stairs, where that larger crack allowed the light to fall onto my mirror when I arrived. Three steps up, a narrow view of the stage reveals itself.

The sun has dipped below the highest gallery of the playhouse, where some of those monkeys sit, fussing over each other and eating, some asleep against pillars or calling down to others in the pit.

I glance back into the darkness below, to see Condell rushing to get his wide arse back into a fresh pair of hose before I can see him.

'It won't be much of a play, without all the lines,' I say, eyes back on the crowd.

'We all know how the stories go, just follow the patterns,' Condell says, 'you enter, you wait and you listen, then you throw in a line or two which you think sounds right according to your part. Make it a rhyme, if you have the time. Keep it short, or have some sport... it doesn't have to be Shakespeare.'

'We don't do too many old plays by Master Shakespeare,' Heminges adds, emerging fully clothed from behind the rack, 'not these days, because whenever we do, the printers send a pair of their pock-faced boys to sit up the back and scribble down our words as best they can. By the time they go to print with it, Will's best poetry sounds like a madhouse ditty!'

Judging it safe to take my eyes from the stage, I say: 'I might have been away from this playhouse for many years, Master Heminges, but I do recall you once had a grand plan to print all the plays of Master Shakespeares in the one book.'

'I did, but then one player of this playhouse took it upon himself to sell the contents of his receptacle to a printer, and when the little books of Master Shakespeares became so popular no printer was interested in paying for our plays anymore, they were only interested in stealing more of them. If I ever discover which player it was I'll hang him by his balls from the top of this playhouse, but I could never catch him at it. I always thought it had to be a player who disappeared from our playhouse, and never dared show his face back here again,' Heminges says.

I glance down at them, three pairs of eyes, looking into me.

Before I can say anything, a sudden round of trumpets announces the play. The crowd explodes into applause.

'We're off!' Condell says.

'No-one is listening to you prattle, Heminges, ready yourself,' Master Burbage says.

'I have, but where is my Lady Montague?' Heminges says, offering the hat and veil to me.

I don them without thinking, and reach for the sliver of mirror in my basket, by the steps, the light from the stage falling across my face.

'Oh dear... I am not ready for this,' I say, pulling the

veil tight and slipping it under my chin.

Heminges takes my arm in a strong grip. 'You'll soon be, duckie. A player who does not play has no place in a playhouse!' he says, as we ascend into the light.

IT IS 1992 and I am on stage with a small dog, feeding it lines from a very long monologue. The crowd is laughing at the blank stares from the little animal, which has a halo of hair like a pom pom.

I'm at the Advanced Residential Theatre and Television Skillcentre (ARTTS) in Yorkshire and we're performing the famous letter scene in Shakespeare's *Twelfth Night*. I am playing the Puritan manservant Malvolio. The dog – a role not written by Shakespeare – is playing the pet of my mistress Olivia.

For weeks the director has made no secret of his desire for the dog to do a shit in this scene. His scenario is this – the long-suffering, righteous Malvolio is mortified that he must take this precocious creature for a walk in his employer's garden. During the outing, he discovers the letter intended to deceive him into thinking his mistress loves him.

I've only worked with the dog a couple of times in rehearsal. It's placid enough, although I am afraid of choking it, since I am tall and the lead is not long enough to allow me to stand upright and project my voice.

The dog is an airhead. The less it gives me in response to the lines in which Malvolio is increasingly drawn into the web of tomfoolery that will be his undoing, the more I give it.

So I pick it up. In a flash I realise that's the way to solve the projection problem, and I realise I can make this bimbo fur-ball into my Lady Olivia.

Completely off the blocking and the timing, I am a creative rogue, and I am stuffing up any chance of the director's vision of me being trumped by a turd. I decide that if the dog shits, I'll treat it like a lump of pure gold.

I end the scene on one knee, the dog aloft in my arms. No shit. The crowd raucously applauds our exit.

Before NIDA was over I knew I wanted to do more than design. The only solution was to go as far away as I could in order to change. So, two months after my mother died at home in her bed I relocated to the far reaches of North Yorkshire where a former pig farm had been converted into an international media school.

Away from the bright lights and big city, there was nothing to do but learn how to produce theatre and screen projects, and the college gave me the opportunity to try something I've been drawn to all my life.

Emboldened by my two terms of acting classes, I campaigned to get cast in the role of Malvolio, and in performance I realised the droll comic potential of the part, to the point that my closet door almost burst open in the process.

I can act, sure, but I'll need to be careful about it.

I'll take to the much larger but less challenging role of loving boyfriend right at the end of my year in Yorkshire, when starting my first relationship, with a woman.

The security and validation that offers will be exactly what I'll need to stay in England and do what Shakespeare did almost four hundred years prior – move from a rural backwater to London and tilting at a career in the performing arts.

Shakespeare succeeded in a very short time, whereas I'll find myself washed up in the corporate video world. Various opportunities to work on films and plays will either come to nothing or fail to launch, and there will be the constant fear and guilt of being closeted.

I'll console myself at the haunts of my favourite writers, from the Brontës' Yorkshire to E. M. Forster's Surrey, and melancholy visits to Stratford-upon-Avon.

I'll give it five years, until I can hide no more. My relationship will dive, my employment contract will be made redundant, and I'll decide it's time to go home to Australia in order to come out.

But I'll discover something interesting underneath my hidden sexuality – Malvolio is just the start.

AS I stumble off the stage, my eyes blinking from all the faces, I stand by the yawning hole of the stairwell. The idea of the darkness again so soon after a bath of afternoon light gives me pause.

But I get myself back down the stairs, remove the hat and veil and check my face in my mirror. With Master Burbage sitting quietly at his table, and Condell plucking at his lute, I become myself again.

'Got your taste for the crowd back, Tooley?' Condell asks.

'I have not been so gazed-upon since I left the playhouse. It has taken away my breath,' I say.

'Aye, but it gives you life,' Condell asserts.

'It does... more than I remember,' I say.

'Are you sure Taylor's up to a whole afternoon's work?' Master Burbage says, 'I could go on for him yet.'

'Let me help you run your lines,' I say, remembering the pages pinned inside his cloak.

Master Burbage holds up a hand. 'Nay, I have conned them all. I am word-perfect, watch.'

He prepares a moment with his back to us, then marks it out.

'Romeo calls at my Apothecary rooms, and I say: "Who calls so loud?". Then he goes on a bit about how poor I am, and offers me forty ducats for a dram of poison, then I say: "Such mortal drugs I have; but Mantua's law is death to any he that utters them," and so on. I know my lines, all of them, and I'll feed Romeo his, when he forgets!'

Surely, while I have been on the stage, he has pinned new play pages inside his cloak, but Condell applauds at the end, and just as I join in, Heminges descends.

'They're right at the top, centre-back, the little upstarts,' he says, stopping at the third step and looking into the crowd.

'Who?' I ask.

'Printer's boys, three of them,' Heminges says. 'I can see their feathers wobbling. There's been two or three 'Romeo and Juliets' stolen by printers over the years. We made a study of their work, as an amusement. How did it go men?'

They all join the poetic drone, accompanied by Condell, impromptu, on the lute:

'Romeo! Romeo! Wherefore are thou roaming now?
Tell thy father and give up thy name;
Or alone alas I will remain.'

'Whatever drivel that springs from our mouths today will be inked as the words of Master William Shakespeare, again,' Heminges says bitterly, removing his hat and loosening his collar.

Left out of the joke, and wondering if indeed it was meant to amuse, I stand between them all, sitting in their corners.

'If it's so very bad, what are you going to do about it, stop the play?' I ask.

Sighing like furnace

IT IS 2003 and I'm heading home to the Blue Mountains after a terrible audition, one of those group calls where the rejected actors get asked to leave after the first round.

I've been catching trains on this line since these carriages were new, and now they're looking a bit shabby. Their shine has gone, just like mine.

Retreat this early means explaining to Jono, my partner of three years, why I'm home by lunchtime with nothing to show for myself.

He knows what show-business is like, having danced, choreographed, acted and directed for two decades, whereas I've never made a splash anywhere.

The journey is giving me too much time to think about all the auditioning I've been doing for months now. Each time, I've caught the train to the city, sought out the shabby rooms above shops or old church halls at the appointed place and time. I've waited with other actors in stairwells, listened in to the auditions before mine, seen the familiar faces of actors who are a bit like me to look at, and we've acknowledged the similarity in silence, knowing they're after a type that only one of us can match.

The last play I was in ran for two weeks, five months ago. It was a Shakespeare of a sort, a production of *The Popular Mechanicals*, an adaptation of the story of the players in Shakespeare's *A Midsummer Night's Dream*. I played Peter Quince, the self-appointed director of a small troupe of mis-matched actors preparing the entertainment for a wedding reception.

I'd followed up news of gigs on the grapevine,

Shakespeare productions for schools, mainly, many of them paid. The first one I did nothing to prepare for, apart from revisiting my *Henry V* monologue from *The Popular Mechanicals*. When asked to 'please do that again, but this time (insert improv specifics here)' (the standard second stage of every audition, meant to identify whether an actor can take direction), I was struck dumb with fear, and simply belted it out exactly as I'd already done it. The actor auditioning with me dropped her gaze to the floor, and I realised even before finishing that I'd completely fucked it up.

Now, months later and halfway home, where the hot Sydney plain surrenders to blue valleys, and the rhythm of the train alters from breakneck speed to gentle, upward rattling, I admit I have no real basis in this industry.

Yet I am just like most actors: I have an agent who does nothing to get me auditions; I am constantly misgauging the auditions I find for myself; and the gap since my last gig – a modelling job in a car commercial – grows embarrassingly long.

I've even tried going back to NIDA, commuting once a week for auditioning classes taught by one of the acting students in my graduation year more than a decade earlier. All traces of my heavily-fringed geek had gone, so he didn't remember me – I'd lost most of my hair, and my shy, retiring act in the interim.

It was through that class I'd heard about my latest, failed audition. I'd done the classical monologue quite well, went a bit better in the modern, but what brought me undone was the impromptu scene reading with an actress.

Before I could really take in the content of the scene, she pressed herself against me, right into my personal space, so close I could smell the hardworking scent of an audition stand-in.

High in the heartland of the Blue Mountains, I ride the shame right on its crest. I am thirty-three years old, I have not managed to create a sustained career, and, silly me, I never anticipated I'd have to play it straight ever again.

I vow to never be so unprepared for another audition, but I am desperate to stop feeling so powerless.

In those lengthy, lonely times between creative opportunities, I'd turned to writing whenever I felt a sense of failure. None of my work had been produced, published or picked up; but surely, I thought, all I needed was to write one great script, and the rest of my career would flow.

Nobody can stop me, I say to myself, buoyant because I already have an idea.

Typically for me, I've been planning my next move and my feet have found their way to a university library in search of a book about John Heminges and Henry Condell, the men who saved half of Shakespeare's plays by publishing them in the one book.

Where the catalogue promised rich detail, the booklet itself revealed scant information. The Civil War, The Great Fire of London, and The Blitz, erased most of the records and places of Shakespeare's time. After a full day of research, through multiple publications, I come to realise that despite many theories, very little is known about how the First Folio was put together. Heminges and Condell are mere ciphers in their own story.

But I am not discouraged. This vacuum is the perfect place for storytelling. I decide to make a start on a first draft by writing every day until it is completed.

MERELY PLAYERS

'THERE'S an idea,' Heminges replies to my suggestion, 'we must stop the play.'

Master Burbage laughs. 'We never stop the play!'

'Bollocks to that, Heminges. We won't get paid,' Condell says, chuckling.

But Heminges is not laughing, I can see his eyes flickering with ideas.

The silence brings Master Burbage to his feet. 'If we stop the play we cannot remind the other shareholders what a fine player Master Tooley is,' he says, making a graceful gesture toward me.

'I don't know about that,' I say, clearing my throat. 'I'm not in very fine voice.'

'Where are we up to?' Heminges demands of us, but his eyes fall on me, so I retreat to the third step and search the stage.

'Capulet's wife and Juliet are not on yet, but soon,' I say.

'We should call a halt after that, and push the pies on the crowd, while Condell and I go up and box those printer's boys around the ears,' Heminges says.

'It is not up to you, Master Heminges, to decide to stop our play,' Master Burbage says, with a final note, one finger upright. 'Come, it's time to see to my face. He could be swarthy, this Apothecary, what do you think?' he adds, easing himself back into his chair.

Out of habit, I move at the same time as Heminges, so that one of us stands either side of Master Burbage.

'I always did my Master's face,' I say.

'I've done his face for him these ten years,' Heminges says.

'Was there no one else to help him?'

'Not after you left,' Heminges says, wryly.

Master Burbage whines as he always did, like a boy: 'I

need my face done. Tooley, where are you?'

'Coming, Master Burbage,' I say. If I don't, I'll end up standing by the costume rack all day.

'The face blacking is in that large pot up the back,' Heminges says, waving a finger at Master Burbage's mess.

'I remember,' I say.

'And there is paper underneath for putting it on,' Heminges says, hovering.

'I see it, thank you Master Heminges,' I say, tucking a cloth around Master Burbage's neck.

The shadows of the players on the stage interrupt our light. Heminges starts to pace. Condell is plucking out a tune on his lute, remembering an old ditty.

'Listen,' Heminges mutters to Condell, 'I have been thinking about how to get us back upstairs.'

I move so that my back is facing them, but I am listening.

Condell sighs, then sings his answer to his tune:
There is no way back upstairs,
We've just got to stop down here
And play whatever they want us to play.'

Heminges cuts him off: 'The parts will run out soon enough. If I must stop playing, I mean to keep getting my share of the takings.'

Condell continues his mock performance:
'Look what happened to Shakespeare
When he stopped playing,
He went to his grave soon enough!'

'The only way to retire on the same money is to make ourselves indispensable to this company by doing something other than playing,' Heminges says.

Condell stops. 'What else can a player do?' he asks.

Heminges whispers his answer. I hear not one word.

Master Burbage is sleeping, his face is like stone until I work it with the sticks of paint.

Condell laughs. 'When the other shareholders find us out, that'll be the end for us. I don't want to go scratching around the cockpits to feed my family. My shares are all I've got, and I'll go on playing for them.'

'When the shareholders find us out they'll clamber over one another for a share of the money,' Heminges says.

'How much?' Condell asks.

'Condell... it would be like jewels instead of glass beads, like venison instead of rabbit. You know how Shakespeare wrote the words.'

Condell considers a moment, then returns to his song.
'Shakespeare's gone to his grave,
If he didn't register any of his copies with the Stationers',
He's only got himself to blame.
Why do you think we were shoved down here
With Burbage?'

'Because the younger men decided we're too old to run the playhouse,' Heminges replies, raising his voice a little too much for his liking.

Condell sings:
'Nay, it's because we made trouble...'

I move so I can see Condell's face. Ceasing to be lyrical, he looks Heminges in the eye.

'Make no mistake, this is the last stop, don't give the shareholders an excuse to show us the door next time,' he says, his face as far from fooling as it could be.

Heminges retreats into the piles of rubbish beyond the shadows, throwing aside boxes and baskets. Condell returns to plucking at the lute strings.

But Heminges is making a terrible noise.

'Perchance you keep it quiet in there Master

Heminges. It is supposed to be a serene night in Verona on the stage,' I say.

'Never fear, they won't hear me from up there, duckie.'

I don't say anything, even though I want to. I need more paper to clean my fingers. There is some under Master Burbage's table.

As I retrieve it, Heminges asks, roughly: 'What's that?'

'What's what?' I reply.

'That paper, in your hand?'

'You told me to use it on Master Burbage's face,' I say.

Before I can pull my hand away, Heminges grabs the papers and shoves them under one of the strips of light, but no matter which way he holds them, he can't read anything.

'This handwriting is so tight, and so covered in face paint, I cannot unravel it. Read it for me,' he demands, holding them out for me:

'Tis now the very witching time of night,
When churchyards yawn and hell itself breathes out
Contagion to this world...'

The commotion wakes Master Burbage, and he completes the lines:

'...now could I drink hot blood,
And do such bitter business as the day
Would quake to look on...'

He laughs: 'Are we doing *Hamlet* again?'

'Is it Shakespeare's lightning hand?' Heminges asks.

I nod my head, because I recognise the scribble. 'Small, malformed, letters... aye, it's Will's writing,' I say.

'Are there any more of these?' Heminges demands.

Before I can say anything, he's pushing his way under the table.

'Heminges, have you forgot yourself?' Master

Burbage asks, standing.

But Heminges ignores him, uncovering a thick pile of papers, handing them to me.

'Read it, quickly,' Heminges says, looking for more.

'A moment...' I say, arms now heavy with paper.

'Is it the other half of *Hamlet*?' Heminges asks.

'I think so,' I reply.

Heminges turns on Master Burbage: 'Where have you been throwing the scraps?'

'On the floor,' Master Burbage replies, refusing to move as Heminges dives for the torn pieces surrounding his chair. 'After that, I take them home, to light my fire.'

'Your fire?' Heminges asks, incredulous.

'Aye. Mrs Burbage finds it cold at night,' Master Burbage says.

'Your fire has been warming Mrs Burbage with some very fine words,' Heminges shouts.

'Don't you speak ill of Mrs Burbage!' Master Burbage says, matching him.

'Quiet, both of you,' I say, knowing the only way to distract Heminges is to tell him what I have seen on the pages. 'Here's *Twelfth Night*, and *King Henry*, and underneath... it appears to be *Othello*.'

'You call yourself players, but if you can't find your words in your receptacles, then you are not up to the job!' Master Burbage says, throwing himself back into his chair.

'What more has already gone up in flames?' Heminges demands, smoothing out scraps of paper. 'Answer me Burbage.'

My Master drops his head, but only for a moment, before throwing up his arms. 'Nobody said you could come down here, into my private room, sniffing around my things, get off, all of you!'

ACTING LIKE SHAKESPEARE REALLY MATTERS

'I have good reason for consulting Will's copy of *Romeo and Juliet*,' Heminges says, grabbing whatever papers he can in the flurry.

'Well, spit it out, we are all shareholders here,' Master Burbage says.

'Is Tooley still a shareholder, after ten years away?' Heminges asks.

But Master Burbage is ready for him: 'We are all shareholders, and though I might have closed my eyes for a moment, I heard you say, John Heminges, that you were planning to take our *Romeo and Juliet* to a printer. Why should we give it to you, knowing you intend to do such a thing?'

'Nay, it was not what you think,' Heminges says, weakly. 'I think there is money to be made, if we players were to talk to a printer ourselves. Good coin, for every man.'

IT is later in 2003 and I am sitting in a bare rehearsal room in western Sydney. Every week, a decent-sized group wanders in after our day jobs. Someone has put the hot water urn on, and we talk about our days.

It's a bit stilted. There is a feeling that functioning adults – trained actors – meeting to work on Shakespeare monologues is something to be ashamed about.

Members of the class sit down one side of the room. Apart from a small door in the wall at the other side, and a few spare chairs, there is not much to disguise this rented suburban warehouse situated within an industrial estate.

Tonight, we're working on the opening monologue of the one-man Chorus in *Henry V*.

We're far enough into the weekly sessions that touches

of courage have started to show. Guided by a director, we've gone from speaking Shakespeare in the requisite posh English that all Australians are drawn to when pronouncing the words of The Bard, to finding the way to play it so we can all understand not just the words, but the emotions.

So, we have secretaries convincing us to imagine the room is the setting of great battles. Customer service representatives have made good on their promises that our imaginations will be enough to see great scenes. Council workers have sat, like boys, with chess sets as props and embodied the Battle of Agincourt for us in a way so powerful that the tiny pieces, and their puppeteer, were the focus of every eye in the room.

When my turn comes, I know not to hesitate or apologise, but to stand my ground and command that I have my say. I'm taking a sarcastic tack, inhabiting the role of jaded studio manager, entrusted to welcome an audience for the recording of a show.

Shakespeare has made it possible. The introduction to his great battle play is interspersed with breaks that allow me to imagine I am being instructed via comms to set the scene, and that I just cannot believe what I am asking these people to imagine.

'Can this cockpit hold the vasty fields of France?'

I say it to an imaginary technical gallery, with disbelief, for this rehearsal room is not half as fine as the stage of London's Globe playhouse, which was plain enough in its day, long before stage design became a big thing.

Immediate laughs. They get it. Because my character doesn't believe what the playwright is expecting the audience to envisage, they don't have to believe it either. It's one way to beg the forgiveness that Shakespeare so cleverly demands.

My *Henry V* monologue ends up being a bit of a one-trick pony, but it is fun.

In a few weeks, I'll be trying something I've never imagined I'd attempt – a monologue from the kind of hero I'd never believed I'd portray: Mark Antony.

I'll delve very deeply into a book I'll purchase for ten cents at a charity shop, written by one of America's great casting directors. His message will sink in easily and quickly: acting is about wanting. Find what the character wants, and get it. Put scores on the board, land the blows.

I'll manage to inhabit the bitter sting of Antony's jealous rage. I'll impart the hurt pride, the kind I am barely willing to express in my everyday life, because I feel it too. I have felt it for years and I will feel it for years to come.

> *'O sun, thy uprise shall I see no more.*
> *Fortune and Antony part here. Even here*
> *Do we shake hands. All come to this? The hearts*
> *That spanieled me at heels, to whom I gave*
> *Their wishes, do discandy, melt their sweets*
> *On blossoming Caesar, and this pine is barked*
> *That overtopped them all. Betrayed I am.*
> *Oh, this false soul of Egypt! This grave charm,*
> *Whose eye becked forth my wars and called them home,*
> *Whose bosom was my crownet, my chief end,*
> *Like a right gypsy hath at fast and loose*
> *Beguiled me to the very heart of loss.'*

I'll manage to impart that Antony feels wronged, and will do almost anything to stop feeling it. There will be his want, blended with my want. There will be Shakespeare's words, blended with my emotions.

I'll be so buried in it that I will not watch for reactions

while I'm acting the scene. I'll only notice, as I come out of character, the startled looks and the discomfort, and I'll know I have learned something about acting, and how want is a necessary ingredient for good writing.

I'll feel confident about all this inner processing, because during these Shakespeare workshops, I will complete the first draft of *Merely Players*.

'I MIGHT have been dreaming, John Heminges, but did I not hear you condemn the player who sold his memory of the plays to a printer?' Master Burbage says.

'I did say it, but this would be different,' Heminges says, standing his ground.

'Oh, this would be *different*?' Master Burbage asks, voice rising.

'Aye, just printing the one play. *Romeo and Juliet*.'

'Heminges, when did you ever read a printed play that was as good as a played one?' Master Burbage asks, ridiculing.

'I don't read plays, as a habit,' Heminges says.

'Nor do I,' Master Burbage says, finding his power, 'and I know Master Tooley never did, and I do believe Master Condell would agree.' Condell nods, tuning his lute. 'That makes no man in this room a fool for reading plays. The printers can never ink a play exactly as we play it, just like we players never play it exactly as the writer wrote it.'

'Are you saying a player is no better than a printer?' Heminges says, not following.

'My brother built this playhouse, from the ground up,' Master Burbage says, pacing by the stairs, 'and none of it, not one splinter, was ever made with a plan of working with an ink-blood like a printer. Plays do not exist on paper, players, they exist in a player's memory, in a playhouse, and nothing more. A printed play is just an excuse for a man to avoid paying to see a play on the stage, and no player should ever wish that on his company.'

Master Burbage's eyes are open wide and wild. Heminges cannot match them, instead he throws himself on the pages at my feet.

'We should have kept a better eye on the copies,' he says. 'Listen to me, all of you, if we want *Romeo and Juliet* to be printed the way Will wrote it, we have got to stop this play.'

'You will not stop this play, not when we have Master Tooley back,' Master Burbage says.

'Why all this fuss about Tooley?' Heminges asks, addressing me. 'Did Burbage get you back with a promise of unpaid shares?'

'Nay, I did not ask it of him,' I reply.

'Where would the company find the coin to pay Tooley for all those years? We've already spent it!' Heminges says.

My Master tries to bring it to an end: 'You heard what he said, he's not come back for the money.'

'What's he come back for then? There won't be too many parts for old women,' Heminges asks.

'He can play out of the skirts, he's done it before,' Master Burbage says.

'I don't want to play out of the skirts,' I say.

'Then no man should get himself worked up,' Master Burbage says, hungry for resolution.

'Tooley is gone ten years, and he's back not five minutes before I catch him with a piece of play in his hand! Next he'll be running off to a printing company with the rest of it!' Heminges says.

'You always made trouble when you didn't get your way,' I say, and it shoots out of me.

'And you always ran off when you didn't get yours,' Heminges fires, just as quickly.

'Sit down Heminges, you need to go over your part,' Master Burbage says, coming between us. 'Tooley, you also. You are Romeo's parents, and you must be ready.'

'I am going to stop this play, whether you like it or not,' Heminges says.

'Not when I am about to go onto the stage,' Condell says, weighing in suddenly.

He retrieves his Fool's hat and lute and mounts the third step to check on the progress of the play. Heminges goes to stop him but Master Burbage holds Heminges by the back of his doublet.

'Quickly Condell, get up there!' Master Burbage shouts.

Condell disappears up into the light, as Heminges wrestles himself free of Master Burbage's grip.

'Tooley, block the stairs!' Master Burbage shouts at me.

I put myself in the way, holding up my fists in the way it feels I ought to, but Heminges easily pushes me aside and I fall against the privy. As I struggle to stand, I see Master Burbage jump on Heminges' back and close his fingers over Heminges' eyes.

'Block the way!' Master Burbage pleads, getting spun around.

'Nay, not while he's thrashing,' I say, cowering.

'Nicholas Tooley, I command you to block the way!' Master Burbage shouts.

'You command me?' I say, seeing only hands and arms flailing.

'I am your Master! I still have your apprentice papers,

signed and sealed, I command you!'

It is the truth, so I block the stairs as he manages to hold Heminges' arms down.

'Heminges, sit down to a rehearsal with Tooley,' Master Burbage shouts.

'You were never my master, Burbage,' Heminges says, running out of breath.

They are standing by the steps, and the light from the stage falls across Master Burbage's eyes.

'Quiet... he starts...' my Master says, reciting what he hears on the stage:

> *'Knock, knock, knock! Who's there, i' th' name of Beelzebub?*
> *Here's a farmer that hanged himself on the expectation of plenty.'*

A loud hammering vibrates through the playhouse frame. 'There's more knocking,' my Master says. 'Knock, knock! Who's there... what was Shakespeare thinking with all that "knock-knock"? Is it supposed to be funny?'

'Is that from *Romeo and Juliet*?' Heminges asks.

'Of course it's not from *Romeo and Juliet*,' Master Burbage says, 'it's the light relief, after Macbeth has murdered the King. "Knock-knock! Who's there?" It's terrible, it'll never make them laugh.'

But a great round of monkey laughter spreads through the crowd. Heminges moves away from the steps.

'Take me back, I want to see the stage!' Master Burbage complains.

And Heminges does, because he has realised something.

'Condell, you're a genius! Look for the printer's boys, are they scribbling?' he asks.

Aye, like mad,' my Master says.

'Excellent work, Condell,' Heminges says with delight.

'He's exiting. He'll be here in a moment,' Master Burbage says, as Heminges throws him roughly off his back.

Condell descends the stairs, his smile as broad as his frame.

'You had me fooled, here I was thinking you weren't behind me, but all the time you were!' Heminges says, clapping Condell on the back. 'Every one of us could do what Condell has done and play any old lines to the printer's boys. Their new *Romeo and Juliet* will be worse than all the others put together. I might do some of my old lines from *Julius Caesar*, what say you, Condell?'

'I fancied I'd fit every Fool I ever played into this *Romeo and Juliet*. What do you wager I can't manage it?' Condell says, pouring himself a drink.

'Enough,' Master Burbage says, rubbing at a sore place on his side. 'Sit down, and keep it quiet. I can see you men are going to play this like little boys. No player is to go off his part again. I am going up to speak to the other shareholders.'

'Nay, Burbage, I'll go,' Heminges says.

'I am the senior shareholder, I am the one to speak to them,' my Master says.

'Tell them our play is being stolen, again,' Heminges demands.

'I'll not be asking them to stop the play, get that idea out of your receptacle. What we need is a meeting of every man, in the alehouse after the play is over, to speak of shares, and our new season, now that Master Tooley has returned to us. If you can find anyone who is interested, you can raise your point about the printer's boys then,' Master Burbage says.

ACTING LIKE SHAKESPEARE REALLY MATTERS

'Are you going to tell them about how Tooley arrays himself?' Heminges asks.

My Master doesn't understand. 'What do you mean?'

'You know what I mean. Is Tooley to come to the alehouse dressed like that?' Heminges asks.

'Of course he won't. He'll have removed all the Montague woman's weeds before,' Master Burbage replies.

'What about what's under the Montague woman's weeds?' Heminges asks.

'Tooley's under the Montague woman's weeds. They'll just have to grow familiar with the weeds,' Master Burbage says.

'Let me come with you,' Heminges says, 'I'll help you with the stairs.'

'Nay, you will stay down here, all of you. Have something to eat.'

IT is 2004 and it's starting to rain as I hit an uncharacteristically lonely stretch of the Princes Highway out of St Peters. I'm in disarray because I needed to leave the dressing room in a hurry.

Jono and I have moved from the Blue Mountains to the southern suburbs of Sydney, replacing a four-hour round trip with a twenty-minute drive.

I usually take the route that runs along Botany Bay, because there's less traffic and an expansive feeling with the great body of water and a huge sky, but this time I want to get home faster because I'm upset. Very upset – I've just been sacked from a production of *King Lear*.

When I auditioned for this production, I noticed the director's interest rise just as I fell to my knees performing one of the droll monologues by the courtier

MERELY PLAYERS

Jacques from *As You Like It*.
> *'Invest me in my motley; give me leave*
> *To speak my mind, and I will through and through*
> *Cleanse the foul body of the infected world,*
> *If they will patiently receive my medicine.'*

My audition technique improved no end after finding that ten-cent book. It worked a treat and I was offered the role of Kent, Lear's faithful servant, finally aware of my niche in Shakespeare.

Never cut out for heroes or fools, I realised with delight the great list of characters like Quince, Malvolio and Jacques – the philosophers, pedants, dreamers and dry wits – whose language was as sarcastic as I could be, with passions every bit as blind. When imbued with great admiration for humanity and the desire for connection that was always beyond them, they made for great theatre moments.

Getting this job was a score, because it was a paid gig, and Jono and I were now paying Sydney rent.

The first week of rehearsals saw everyone co-opted into detailed sessions of transposing the text, during which the director made no secret of her willingness to be open to ideas from the actors.

Then I had an idea. My character, Kent, is a loyal friend to the King, and spends the bulk of the play in disguise. Having cast all Shakespeare's male characters as female, the director had interestingly changed the power structure of *King Lear*, but there was one thing she didn't do – my role was male in Shakespeare's original, and remained male in this new vision. Why?

That's where my idea came in – if being female meant access to power and security in this director's vision, then surely, I thought, Kent should disguise himself as a woman in this production.

ACTING LIKE SHAKESPEARE REALLY MATTERS

It would add to the comic possibilities, but, like Max Klinger in *M*A*S*H*, the cross-dressing could also be for a purpose that wasn't entirely funny.

Far from being dismissed, the idea was pondered and eventually approved. I hasten to add it scared me shitless – I am not a man who would ever pass convincingly as a woman, and so my courageous offer would need some rationale, some device from within this interesting world, to support my disguise, which was an unchangeable plot point of Shakespeare's play. It would certainly need an effective costume.

So I placed complete trust in this director, donned a rehearsal skirt, and experimented with my voice and my character's journey.

We were put through our paces by a fight director, daily, to achieve complicated sword fighting sequences. Seeing empowered women wielding swords in pivotal Shakespearean roles was an amazing experience.

Conversely, seeing Lear's daughters – sketchily drawn as bitchy and evil – played by men, was fascinating.

Many of the cast had been selected for their stage fighting skills and experience. A few of us were totally new to the discipline, so we trained from the ground up. Nevertheless, the cast quickly fell into two groups: the 'Fight Club', and the rest of us who were learning to execute the moves.

At last came the moment when the costume designer co-ordinated fittings, and his vision for this female-dominated world would surely include a costume to assist in making my idea work within the world of the play.

My excitement quickly turned to dread when he produced a dress which I could tell immediately I was never going to fit into. Vainly, I tried, and it ripped, but by that time the designer had walked away, seemingly uninterested in what I would be wearing for ninety per cent of the play.

But production stresses were kicking-in and the director became unapproachable. Having been a director, I decided that what she'd appreciate the most was a proactive actor who'd sort out his own costume issues for himself.

Being a trained costume designer, I simply replicated what the designer had created for the female characters in the production, so well in fact that even he would have to admit it fitted into the world of the play seamlessly – forget that he wasn't really doing his job until he'd adequately costumed me.

Before the great theatrical sin I'd committed was voiced, I also spent time ensuring that dangerous backstage conditions were sorted out, not by complaining at notes sessions, but by proactively recruiting fellow cast members into helping me move the sharp metal stair treads that had been dumped across the main backstage exit, waiting to impale someone in the dark.

I also tried to bridge the growing gap between the cast (who were expected to assemble bleacher seating before dress runs) and the crew (who were under great stress as difficult set elements were wrangled). I knew that whinging actors were no help to this scenario.

But when the producer (who'd recently given birth and had her attentions split so many ways she was hardly there) spat at the cast saying we should be thankful we were being paid, I responded by asserting that it wasn't helpful to put things that way.

A kind of calm descended on the company at that point – we had a schools' matinee to perform, and the auditorium filled with hundreds of raucous students, hungry for entertainment.

ACTING LIKE SHAKESPEARE REALLY MATTERS

The show opened, I executed my disguise scene in good time, and we went into the first major fight sequence, in which Kent makes a desperate attempt to escape capture.

I had one move to execute which the fight director encouraged me to compare to teeing off on a golf course – a 360-degree swing which was Kent's attempt to slit the throat of his opponent who was prone on the floor. If it was golf, the way this move was choreographed would have seen the ball fly off into the audience.

And that's exactly what my sword did, after the tip clipped the floor and the choreographed force of the swing behind it sent the weapon right out of my sweaty hands.

In dread, I watched as the silver spike glinted in the darkness high above the heads of the amazed schoolboys, who were surely thinking: *This is supposed to happen, right?*

I had immediate visions of being arrested for injuring children, as all eyes in the room watched the sword descend, and a small boy – the hero of the day – stood and simply caught the blade as it flew towards his head, just like a football.

Speechless, I led a standing ovation for the kid who'd saved my arse, and called him to the stage to return the sword to my hand – all in character, I hasten to add – and then returned to the fight, which was only half over.

When I stumbled off the stage minutes later, some of my non-Fight Club comrades were desperate to know what had happened. I implored them to just soldier on.

We went through the Q&A session with students and teachers afterwards, at which the amazing stunts the gathered crowd had participated in were congratulated. I left it to the director and the fight director to explain.

They declined, po-faced. The schools left, and we started de-mobbing the show, when I got a call to meet the director in the upper foyer.

As I approached I could hear her speaking. Thinking someone was being seen before me, I slowed down, only to see her rehearsing something to an imaginary other. Then it dawned on me – I was the imaginary other.

I cleared my throat, and gently knocked.

I don't know whether it was my courageous act of completing my own costume, to make sense of what I was doing in the confusing world the director was struggling to birth, or whether it was the impromptu thrills of my sword throwing, but I was summarily sacked.

I was quite calm and just asked her to explain how the costume she wanted me to wear fit into the world of the play, let alone across my torso?

She was incapable of speaking, from anger, from fatigue and confusion. This was a useless moment that would never find an answer, because the director had lost touch with the fundamental questions that were integral to her role. None of my attempts to help amounted to anything but rebellion, and I'd unwittingly opened the doorway to the kind of shame and negative attention endured by cross-dressers for centuries.

I walked through the theatre back to the dressing room. The rest of the cast sat in a notes session on the stage. When some friends among them looked to me, their eyes querying, I indicated I was off the show by gesticulating a cut throat, collected my things from the dressing room, and took to the road.

Jono shrugged and laughed when I told him, later that night, about my sacking. It was probably the most creative day of my entire life, and he let me complain about the injustice of it all, but we'd already developed a special way of making light of the disappointments of show-business, and he taught me to move on quickly.

By the end of that night I already knew what I would be moving on to – a second draft of *Merely Players*.

CONDELL has already started eating from the pie basket and offers it around. Heminges willingly takes one, unwrapping the paper and using it to wipe his mouth as he eats, but I am not hungry.

'One of us should have gone with Burbage,' Heminges says, chewing.

'You mean to say you should have gone with him,' I say.

'I am only trying to help all of us,' Heminges complains.

'There is one thing that has not changed in all the years I was away,' I say.

All that comes back at me is the sound of men eating, while I straighten the room.

'Where were you these many seasons?' Heminges finally asks.

'You probably never noticed how much it pained me, to sit and watch you all on the stage, with the younger boys playing in my old finery,' I say, keeping my eyes off him.

'Now I remember, there was that problem with the new boy player,' Heminges says, his mouth full.

'The problem was not with the boy, the problem was with the mother,' I say.

'It's worse now, we cannot have a hint of sodomy about the playhouse,' Heminges says.

'I never touched him,' I say, on top of a sigh.

'They'll shut us down if they think we're harbouring sodomites,' Heminges says.

'Sometimes, the new boys took it badly when I showed them how to strap themselves down, in between their legs, but that little shyte said something about it to its mama. She cried like a Puritan, calling sodomy at what she did not understand,' I say.

'But something must have made you leave, Tooley,' Condell says, swallowing.

I have become still, my back to them. This is the moment I have played in my head so many times, these ten years. I have left it so long I barely remember my reasons.

'Cleopatra was the last role Shakespeare wrote for me,' I say. 'I stayed for a season after that, and I tried playing out of the skirts, but I found that I could not. I took myself away. I admit I saw some very black days. Eventually I was taken in by the good women at the Convent of Saint Helen, and they saved me from the very worst.'

'I stopped sending your coin, after the nuns sent it back. We all agreed that meant you must have gone to your grave,' Heminges says.

'In a way, I had,' I say.

They let my point lie on the earthen floor between us.

'Well, you'll just have to muck in as best you can, until all the shareholders have decided what coin there will be for you,' Heminges says.

'I will take no coin when I haven't played for it,' I say, angrier than I want it to be.

'You might have to stick to that plan, Tooley,' Heminges says, laughing. 'Paying full shares for old men playing just one or two roles is the fastest way to drive a company of players into the ground.'

ACTING LIKE SHAKESPEARE REALLY MATTERS

'That's the way it was when old Master Armin was still with us,' Condell says. 'I played all the big roles, and he did the small, but we got paid the same. It was like that until we had to carry him off the stage to his last bed, and that's the way it's going to be until they come down here and carry me to mine.'

'Even a fool could see there are too many shareholders already,' Heminges says to his pie.

Condell takes it badly. 'Are you calling me a fool, on the stage, and off?'

'Aye, if you cannot see that more shareholders means less money for all of us,' Heminges replies.

'Master Heminges' habit of calling other players fools is what got us down here,' Condell says, glumly.

'When this playhouse needed new players, I only pointed out that no young player who thought anything of himself would become a shareholder of the Globe playhouse, when all we older players were kept on, unless we gave them something else to make them feel important,' Heminges explains. 'I only suggested they be allowed to attire themselves closer to the stage. It was a brilliant idea.'

'So brilliant they moved Burbage down here a month later, with us following this season,' Condell adds.

It forces the most bitter retort from Heminges: 'You might think there is no way back upstairs, Condell, but I do.'

They fall silent, eating possible answers down. I use the break to ask: 'Is Master Burbage quite well?'

'Aye, you've seen him,' Heminges replies.

'But on the stage, he is like he always was?'

'He always makes a big show of handing over his role to one of the younger men, then he swears he's not going on in the small part they give him,' Condell says. 'We just play along with it, because when it comes to it, he goes on, and he sends the crowd into a passion in even the smallest part. You could get your taste for it again. If any of the boys cannot go on, you can stand in.'

That breaks Heminges' anger, and on a laugh he says: 'Join us, forever waiting for one of the lads to come down with the French Pox and give us an afternoon's work.'

Condell chortles and finishes off his pie by opening the paper and licking the insides. The way the light falls through it, Heminges and I notice the lettering on the wrapping at the same time. Offended, Condell rolls his eyes, but Heminges grabs the paper.

'What's here? I can't read it.'

Condell laughs. 'You're seeing Shakespeare's hand everywhere now Heminges.'

'Read it!' Heminges demands.

Condell complies:

'Alack, 'tis he: why, he was met even now
As mad as the vex'd sea; singing aloud;
Crown'd with rank fumiter and furrow-weeds...'

I recognise the verse, and finish it:

'With bur-docks, hemlock, nettles, cuckoo-flowers,
Darnel, and all the idle weeds that grow
In our sustaining corn...'

I tell them: 'It is from *King Lear*, the daughter, Cordelia.'

'Are there more?' Heminges asks, diving into the pie basket and pulling at wrappings, 'is it all the same hand?'

'Aye, it's Will's,' I say.

'Condell, get to the bakery, see what is left,' Heminges demands.

'I'll go when the play is over.'

'You'll go now, before they sell more pies wrapped in *King Lear*. None of us is needed on the stage. Get to the bakery and bring all the paper you can find up there,' Heminges says.

Condell sighs, shrugs and makes for the steps.

'Gather everything off the floor, every scrap, however small,' Heminges says, enlisting me.

It is my chance to speak with him alone, so I submit to sorting the plays into piles at the centre of the room. We work swiftly together, in silence, Heminges flattening pie wrappings and shaking his head from time to time.

'I fear my coming back has got you all dancing around like rabbits,' I say, drawing him out.

'We haven't had so much to dance about of late,' Heminges says, distracted. 'This looks like *Julius Caesar*, do you have more of Caesar?'

'This pile here is all Caesar,' I reply, taking the sheets from him. 'Is it also my women's weeds?'

'Why would any player think less of another player attired in women's weeds?'

'Because I won't be taking them off, when I leave here tonight,' I reply, cautiously.

'But you are the same Tooley as was,' he says, dismissively, then, holding out a page spattered with food: 'Can you make this out?'

I read, reaching into my memory. 'It's from The Dream,' I say, finding the right pile, before saying: 'I'm not entirely the same.'

'You are still a man, when it comes to it, I suppose we can prove that, if the Puritans make a fuss about you,' Heminges says. 'Here's more bits of *Hamlet*. They're torn but you can make out the words.'

'You need not think of me that way, Heminges. I passed for a woman to the nuns.'

But he is lost in pages, holding out a bunch of them. 'More of *Hamlet*, I think.'

'A woman knows when a man is not listening to what she is saying,' I say, wryly.

'Aye, you're sounding more like Mrs Heminges, the more you prattle,' Heminges says, emptying out the pie basket on the floor.

'Then you'll get used to me, in time,' I say, knowing he is watching me.

'I remember when you first came to the playhouse, and you were a boy, like every other. The women's weeds were only for the stage. Why did you change?'

I cannot look at him. 'What are those pages at your feet?'

Heminges reads with great difficulty, using a shaft of light to see anything:

'O, then, I see Queen Mab hath been with you.
She is the fairies' midwife...'

'It's more fairies from The Dream,' he decides.

'You are not the same as you were in those days,' I say.

'Aha! It's not The Dream,' Heminges says, with sudden animation. 'I played him once, it's Mercutio from *Romeo and Juliet*!'

'You've grown to be less sure of yourself, and you find it harder to read the roles,' I say.

'Bollocks. We might all be changed men, but none has changed as much as you,' Heminges says. Then, holding it out like a prize: 'Only one page of *Romeo and Juliet*? Well, it's a start, there will be more in here, and I'll find it.'

Condell comes briskly down the stairs, a large pile of papers in his arms.

'Saved, saved from the greasy fingers of bakers' tarts,' he says, putting them down next to my organised piles, messing them a little. 'They had all this stashed in the corner holding up a butter churn, and when I asked if there was more, they stared and blinked at me, as though I was a horse who'd thought to start speaking. One of them piped up and said that they "could nawt rememba whan the paypers cayme". Top of the pile is a slice of Will's Tempest! When I took these from their greasy little fingers, the chatty one had the hide to ask me if I was "gaarn to brang some back to wrap tamorraw's poyes!".'

'Tooley, see if there is anything of *Romeo and Juliet* in there,' Heminges says.

I start to search as Condell sits and eats one of the unwrapped pies.

'Tomorrow's pies! She wanted to wrap tomorrow's pies in the only copy of Will Shakespeare's Tempest!' Condell says.

'Perchance you both see our problem better now?' Heminges asks.

'Aye, although I admit I always thought Will Shakespeare's plays were a little overcooked,' Condell says, setting himself off laughing.

'It's most of *The Tempest*,' I report, getting Heminges' immediate attention. 'The rest is *As You Like It* and *Antony and Cleopatra*, and something else...'

'Read it,' Heminges demands.

I clear my throat, grappling with unfamiliar verse:
'If we say that we have no sin, we deceive ourselves, and there is no truth in us.
Why, then, belike we must sin, and so consequently die:
Ay, we must die an everlasting death.
What doctrine call you this, Che sera, sera, What will be, shall be? Divinity, adieu!'

All three of us discover the answer at the same time: 'Christopher Marlowe!'

'Give that rubbish back to the baker's tarts,'

Heminges says, 'or even better, write on the back of it. We need some paper, but we'll also need some ink.'

'What for?' I ask.

'When Burbage comes back, we've got to sit him down and get him remembering Romeo's big speeches. You can write them on the back of Marlowe.'

'Don't vex him before he goes on as the Apothecary,' I say. 'Wait until the play is over, when he's gathered his wits.'

'That will be too late. I only want a handful of pages from *Romeo and Juliet* to take to the Stationers Guild. It's in Burbage's head and I want to get it out. Perchance you want to spend the time on some other matter, Tooley?' Heminges asks. 'If the company is going to honour your shares, we could see this as your way of earning them. Fetch some inks.'

'I have no interest in my shares, Heminges,' I say, my voice plain with truth.

'All we have heard from you today, Master Tooley, are the many reasons you're not here,' Heminges says, his sarcasm reaching a peak. 'You're not here to play, yet you're playing. You're not here to reclaim your shares, yet you've allowed Burbage to go and make representations to the other shareholders on your behalf. While you're working out why you are here, I am asking you to act as scribe for a pressing matter which I believe will be of benefit to the older men in our company. If that is so very objectionable to you, duckie, I think it's time for you to be on your way.'

In truth I do not know what my Master will find when he comes back down the stairs, but I know I must be here if he needs me.

'Alright,' I reply. 'I'll scribe for you, but just a few of his big speeches, and you'll go easy.'

ACTING LIKE SHAKESPEARE REALLY MATTERS

'I was still hoping we'd get to the alehouse early,' Condell says, disconsolate.

'You can sit and start scribing what they're playing on the stage, while the rest of us go back and remember what's been played so far,' Heminges says, starting to pace. 'Where is Burbage? We need him back down here, and we need to find some ink in this mess.'

'Master Burbage always keeps bottled blood, if I recall,' I offer.

'It will do.'

'I'll craft some quills,' I say.

'My thanks to you, Master Tooley,' Heminges says, as though relieved to have some action out of me, at last.

There are feathers on one of the hats on the rack and from them I start to cut two quills. The stool will serve as my tablet, while Heminges retrieves a bottle of blood from Burbage's mess and makes two portions, one for Condell and one for me.

Condell has set himself up with a chair on the third step, with a view of the stage, and, happy to sit, drink, and eat, he begins scribing what he sees on the stage.

IT is later in 2004 and although my life has completely altered, I'm sitting in a brand new kitchen, trying to put something into words for my best friend.

On the last day of May, just a few weeks before, Jono died on the rehearsal room floor. Right now, they don't know his cause of death. The Glebe Mortuary has samples of his tissues, taken during the post mortem, and they're being subjected to toxicology.

He and one of the cast of his new show were doing dance moves at the back of another dance class, warming up before their own rehearsal in the next room.

Jono had complained of a racing heart, so he sent his colleague on a break. By the time she returned five minutes later, he'd collapsed on the floor. Two members of staff tried to resuscitate him, but he was declared dead on arrival at the hospital.

He was only forty-four.

I am staying in the Blue Mountains. My best friend has asked me to come and live with her young family. I am not sure I should, but I am running out of options.

I've discovered that Jono's relatives are in the process of disenfranchising me from his estate. His latest show is not going ahead. I have no job and city rent to pay. I am afraid in my own home. Life is a complete mess, but I can't admit to it or I will cease functioning altogether.

My friend is wrangling the dirty dishes and I am trying to articulate something about gay and lesbian equality. I am not entirely clear what I want to say and she is not really listening to me, because I'm expressing things that have never come out of my mouth, things that have never crossed my mind.

My heart is paralysed – again – with a sense of failure.

In the weeks before Jono's sudden death, I'd been writing the second draft of *Merely Players*. I was only three scenes in, but the work I'd completed on the character of Nicholas Tooley included fleshing out his transgender identity. Even in the first draft, he was the most disenfranchised of the characters.

Jono had asked me to sit at our kitchen table and share the story with him. He generously predicted it could be a great backstage comedy – his favourite genre – and we agreed how well comedy sits alongside tragic themes.

But I realise my best friend cannot replace the

presence of my show-business touchstone, my husband. I'm trying to say a play would be a good place to put some of these emotions I am feeling, but really, I have no confidence about whether the unfolding drama will allow me to ever recapture the peace and security required to get back to writing it.

Seeking the bubble reputation

'WHAT DID THE shareholders say?' Heminges asks, the first of us to spot Master Burbage as he returns.

'Shareholders?' my Master replies, looking over the piles of papers.

'Will they meet with us today?' Heminges asks.

Burbage chews his lips and looks across the papers again, quizzically. 'They laugh when it's a comedy, and they cry when it's a tragedy...' he says.

Misunderstanding, Heminges says: 'Aye, that's what brings in the money. What did they say Burbage?'

'He didn't do it,' Condell ventures, quietly.

'Methinks he had not the audience he wanted,' Heminges adds.

'Doesn't want to admit it,' Condell says, sniggering.

'Where are we up to?' Master Burbage booms at them.

Condell peers onto the stage. 'Juliet's father is speaking with her,' he says. 'Very sternly.'

'Burbage, I want you to recite all Romeo's big speeches,' Heminges says. 'Tooley will scribe for you.'

'I know all my big speeches, I don't need them written down.'

'The balcony scene would be a very good start,' Heminges says.

'You want me to say it, without anyone here to see it?' Master Burbage says.

Heminges laughs. 'Here's your chance to play Romeo this afternoon, old man.'

'I think perchance you are addled in your head,' my Master says. 'I only say the play when there is a crowd before me, and they've paid their pennies to see it.'

ACTING LIKE SHAKESPEARE REALLY MATTERS

'Aye, that's what we usually do, but today we need to do something a little out of the ordinary,' Heminges says.

'Why?' my Master asks, blocked from getting back to his chair by the piles of play I did not intend to put in his way.

'Because *Romeo and Juliet* is being stolen, again, and Will's copy seems to have gone up in flames in Mrs Burbage's parlour fire, or been cooked in the Globe playhouse bakery!' Heminges answers.

'It's all in here, in my receptacle,' Master Burbage says, tapping the side of his head. 'It cannot be stolen.'

But Heminges is ready for his objections. 'Aye, that's what we all believed, until today, yet stolen this play will be if we let it finish and we do nothing. Just regale us with a little of your memory, Burbage.'

'My memory?' Master Burbage says, incredulous.

'Aye, remind us what a good play *Romeo and Juliet* was,' Heminges says, his eyes suddenly falling on me.

I take my cue, trying to appear helpful. 'Start with the balcony scene,' I suggest.

'Balcony?' my Master says, confused.

'I'm up top, but I don't see you climb up,' I explain.

'Oh aye... aye...' Master Burbage says, then adds:
  'But, soft! what light through yonder window breaks?'

'That's it,' I say, encouraging him to continue:
  'It is the east, and Juliet is the sun.
  Arise, fair sun, and kill the envious moon,
  Who is...'

But his lower jaw trembles in silence.

'Run at it again, straight away,' Heminges says.
  'But, soft! what light through yonder window breaks?
  It is the east, and Juliet is the sun.
  Arise, fair sun, and kill the envious moon.'

Burbage finishes with a flourish of his hands, looking

very pleased with himself.

'Now, the rest,' I say, which causes my Master to drop his pose. I catch the pained look in his face.

'A pause, I think,' I say to Heminges.

'A pause, after only... three lines?' Heminges asks.

'Aye, a moment.'

'Alright, but we must get on with it,' Heminges says.

My master seems frozen, until I take him by the shoulders and lead him around the piles of play pages to his chair. I fetch a drink from Condell's barrel. Heminges is looking over Condell's shoulder as he sits on the third step, watching the action on the stage.

'Are you getting it down?' Heminges asks.

'Aye, in bits,' Condell answers.

'Show me.'

'Get me a drink first, it'll flow better with something inside me,' Condell says.

I dodge Heminges as he fills Condell's cup from the barrel. 'Let me see it,' Heminges says, offering the drink in exchange for the pages.

My master drinks from his cup like a suckling babe, as Condell offers up one page.

Heminges brings it to his face under a crack in the stage floor above. 'Is that the best you can do?' he asks.

'What's wrong with it?' Condell complains.

'Well, it's hard to follow,' Heminges says.

'That'll be your bad eyes,' Condell says.

'There's nothing wrong with my eyes. Why are you writing it across the page?'

'To fit it all in!'

'Write down the page, and put every character's name in large letters, so it can be seen. Are you putting in the pauses and the gestures?'

'No,' Condell says.

'Well, catch them, otherwise the poetry won't come across,' Heminges says.

'If you want poetry, you'll have to pay a scribe.'

'Just do it better,' Heminges says, handing the page back to Condell and calling to me. 'Come, get him back, we must press on.'

I use my sleeve to wipe the sweat from my Master's brow, help him to stand and bring him back to the centre of the room.

'Ready now... run at it, then all the way through. Juliet is up there, waiting for you, though she does not see you, her Romeo,' I say.

But my Master rushes through it:

'But, soft! what light through yonder window breaks?
It is the east, and Juliet is the sun.
Arise, fair sun, and kill the envious moon...'

He extends the last word, as though that will bring the next phrase to him.

'He doesn't have it,' Condell says.

'I have it!' Master Burbage says, bellowing:

'But, soft! what light through yonder window breaks?
It is the east, and Juliet is the sun.
Arise...'

This time a strange noise comes from my Master's throat, a song of anger and pride. 'Why will anyone want to read it?' he asks.

'Dickie...' I say, but he cuts me off.

'None will want to read it!' Master Burbage says, stamping.

'He doesn't have it,' Condell says, shrugging.

'Silence!' Master Burbage says.

I don't know what else to do but take him back to his chair. The other men are whispering, but I catch every word.

'You know what it's like when it doesn't flow and every man can see it,' Heminges says.

'Aye, but his well seems to have run completely dry!' Condell says.

'He can still do it. They haven't taken him off the stage, they wouldn't dare!' Heminges says.

'He is getting much lesser roles now,' Condell says. 'It matters not if he prattles bits of this and that, he knows what carriage to put behind it. Then you come along and ask him to say Romeo's words, but he cannot remember more than three lines! Take my advice, Heminges, just leave all this and let's go to the alehouse early...'

'Nay, not until we have enough to show the stationers,' Heminges says, trying to get my attention. 'Tooley, you realise what we are trying to do here?'

I leave my Master and cross to the stairs. 'I do, but you're going about it in the wrong way.'

'Oh?' Heminges says.

IT is 2005 and I am not writing anything, I'm raking leaves with Nina in her garden. Nina lives alone, just around the corner from where I am living in a granny flat at the back of a friend's house, a block from where I grew up in the Blue Mountains.

Nina loves to rake the leaves. She rakes them up one end of the lawn, and then she rakes them back the other way.

The first day we met, it was only after we had the same conversation three times that I came to terms with Nina's dementia. The aged-care company I work for didn't always warn carers of the full extent of the condition of the clients we regularly visit, but I'd had a little bit of training in recognising the signs and giving proper care.

The second day I came, Nina was sitting at the small table by her back door, in her coat and hat, her handbag on her lap. She crossed to the passenger side of my car before I could prevent her getting in.

'We're going shopping,' she said through the open window.

'We are,' I replied, 'but it's a little bit too early Nina.'

'Is it?' she asked.

'We need to do some gardening first,' I pretended.

'We do?' she asked.

'Yes,' I replied.

'It's warm in the sun, and cool in the shade,' she said.

'It is,' I replied.

Satisfied that all was in order, Nina acquiesced, and we went inside.

Dementia clients are permitted to stay in their own homes if they have family to check on them, and the week before, I'd met Nina's daughter who lives a short walk away. She'd told me about the day, many years ago, when Nina had taken her grandchildren to the cinema at a shopping centre for a matinee.

Before the screening, the children lost their grandmother. She had transitioned from a functioning person into a dementia client in one lost moment, and although she was found, Nina never appeared to have returned.

But enough is understood about dementia for us to know sufferers are present, despite appearances. Every time we rake the leaves, Nina will say at least once: 'It's warm in the sun, and cool in the shade,' and I casually agree. It fills her with the comfort of knowledge, and sets her on her course, until next time.

MERELY PLAYERS

At another client's home, his living space had surrendered to the equipment of his care needs – oxygen tanks and walking frames presided over entire walls of books, and the enormous dining table was covered in paperwork, so that at first glance he seemed to be a working academic.

In the wonderful mess, I spotted the care plan in its familiar folder, at the edge of the piles of paperwork.

He stalked in front of the fireplace and asked when he would be able to light it. There were no logs, no kindling, no matches. My manager had not told me much about this client either, so I waited to see if we'd have the same conversation three times.

We did.

When I asked him if he'd like some lunch, he walked to his paperwork, looking patiently through the folders, the top of which sported large black lettering. I read 'Mornings', 'Evenings', 'Getting Dressed' and 'Toilet'. He scanned through until he found 'Lunch', giving an embarrassed laugh, as though his ruse was discovered.

But it was not a ruse. That pile of paperwork was the missing contents of his brain. I realised, standing in the large central room of the old Mountains mansion, that this elderly man I'd been sent to care for was the embodiment of Richard Burbage.

The bright green polo shirt I must wear on my shifts is a constant reminder of where my life has taken me – back to the town I grew up in, frustrating me with an overbearing sense of thwarted dreams, into the only kind of employment I can manage in my deepest grief.

I don't mind the work. It gets me out of my head, and I have plenty to escape from. Jono's relatives have removed me from his death certificate and are preventing me from creating his estate. They denied we were in a relationship. They even denied they knew he was gay.

Often, during my care shifts, I witness incredible acts of courage from older people, and equally extreme acts of cowardice. It's an eye-opening time for me, and I feel as far from creativity as it's possible to be.

Which is why I will refuse to give up acting. I've recently finished one play and I will soon be in the middle of another show. This time, I will play my first Shakespearean lead role – Petruchio in *The Taming of the Shrew* – and I will transform myself from a grief-stricken loser into a romantic hero.

Three times a week, I will join the cast by the river at Emu Plains, where we'll join other casts by other rivers, bays and parks, playing Summer Shakespeare on light-filled, languid, evenings under skies darkened only by flocks of fruit bats on their way to feed.

We will draw the kind of crowds I have never before played to, enormous and full of expectation. I will match their energy by running up the hillside from the river bank with a wave of chaos that will fill every ear, but will take its toll on me.

Inside, I will be a broken man playing a self-confident arsehole. It'll be an exquisite dodge, executing physical comedy like an expert, keeping myself and everyone else off the scent of my pain, acting the self-actualised Italian machismo of Petruchio. Nobody will dare to ask me a question. I'll get to talk over the crowd and run the show, at the same time as my entire life is being picked over in the most unwelcome analysis of litigation, and I'll be doing it all without the support of my partner.

But I'll find solace in Nina's garden. She keeps things very simple there. If she wants a change of scene, she disappears inside, sometimes dodging me altogether. I always know where she is when she starts up on the piano, playing old tunes and singing with sudden gusto.

She cannot cook herself a meal, or communicate with her grandchildren, but Nina can recall entire sets of old songs with indelible force. A person reaching for a lost memory looks the same as an actor reaching for a line.

'YOU cannot throw a man into the middle of a play, and expect him to find his way,' I say. 'A play is not for carrying by one man only. Feed it into him, and that will draw him out.'

'Aha, yes. You see Condell, we only have to draw him out,' Heminges says. 'Come, what is the scene?'

'Capulet's orchard,' I reply.

'Write that down,' Heminges says. 'Now, what do we see?'

'Juliet is on the balcony,' I reply.

'Aha, yes. Write that in too. We need a Juliet,' Heminges says. 'Both of you, keep writing. I'll be the Juliet.'

He disappears into the shadows by the stairs and drags out a large basket and stands on it, nearly hitting his head on the low beams above.

'You're but four and ten years old, arrayed by your mother,' I say, but it comes out droll.

Heminges spooks for a moment, then recovers. 'Assume I am in the garments. The age you'll just have to forgive. What am I doing?'

'You've just met Romeo for the first time,' I say.

'Ah, that's you Burbage. I've met you and I have fallen for you,' Heminges says.

'Ha!' my Master says, from the edge of the game.

'She's not fallen, not yet,' I add. 'She's only... thinking about him at this point.'

ACTING LIKE SHAKESPEARE REALLY MATTERS

'Aye, I'm thinking about my Romeo,' Heminges sings, one careless hand on a hip, the other at the side of his face, and his eyes fluttering upwards.

'She is supposed to be so beautiful that the moon would be envious to shine upon her,' I say.

'Well, use your imagination,' Heminges says. 'Come, my Romeo.'

Burbage starts the lines from his chair, and works his words into magic:

> *'But, soft! what light through yonder window breaks?*
> *It is the east, and Juliet is the sun.*
> *Arise, fair sun, and kill the envious moon,*
> *Who is already sick and pale with grief,*
> *That thou her maid art far more fair than she...'*

But the bitter silence hangs on his lips, yet again.

'Did you get it?' Heminges asks.

'Aye,' I say, writing on the page.

'You were right, he remembered more of it. Try again, Burbage,' Heminges says, at the peak of his empathy.

My Master bursts into life again:

> *'Angels and ministers of grace defend us!*
> *Be thou a spirit of health or goblin damn'd,*
> *Bring with thee airs from heaven or blasts from hell,*
> *Be thy intents wicked or charitable...'*

Heminges eyes fall on me. I shake my head.

'That's not Romeo, is it?' Heminges says, but Burbage has more:

> *'I'll call thee Hamlet,*
> *King, father, royal Dane: O, answer me!*
> *Let me not burst in ignorance; but tell...'*

Heminges overrides him. 'You have the wrong play, Burbage, we need Romeo.'

'Go and see Master Shakespeare, and ask him to give

you the words,' my Master shouts, and turns away in his chair.

The stillness in the tight, darkening space is immediate. Even the beams have stopped groaning, as though the whole building, the players on the stage, and every monkey in the crowd, has heard the name William Shakespeare mentioned once again, three years after his death in faraway Stratford-upon-Avon.

'But, Master Shakespeare is gone to his grave,' Heminges says.

'Nay, Master Shakespeare's gone to the country to write me another play,' my Master insists.

'Burbage, you know very well that Shakespeare has been dead these three years,' Heminges says, tapping his hands together, testing the mood.

But my Master is convinced. 'He's going to write me a role for an old foolish King, who spoils with his children.'

'That was *King Lear*,' Heminges says, clipping his words while keeping their edges soft. 'It is already written.'

'Will's only stalling for time,' Master Burbage assures, adjusting his collar. 'Meanwhile, we're to put together a season. Master Tooley is returned, and we'll get all the Lord Chamberlain's Men back to the playhouse now.'

Heminges moves in swiftly. 'They haven't called us the Lord Chamberlain's Men these many years, not since the Queen went to her grave,' he says. 'We are the King's Men now, remember?'

It has no impact on Master Burbage, so Heminges dives for the remnants of the play and holds them firmly under my Master's nose.

'Here is *King Lear*, already on the page, and already played on the stage,' Heminges says.

ACTING LIKE SHAKESPEARE REALLY MATTERS

Standing back by the costume rack, I say, softly: 'You were the King in that one Dickie.'

'I was?'

'You were a fine King. It was long ago now,' I say.

The playhouse breathes out, and the beams begin to groan again. The distant voices of players on the stage return, as my Master finally speaks.

'They laugh when it's a comedy, and they cry when it's a tragedy...'

Finally comprehending, I say: 'Aye, come, lie yourself down.'

My master looks up into my eyes, nodding, before leaning back in order to sleep.

Condell is the first to mutter: 'He is past it, Heminges. No more.'

'Nay, you saw him, Hamlet was flowing out of him like a spring!' Heminges says.

As it reaches my ears, I say: 'My Master must restore himself before he goes onto the stage. Where are we up to?'

Condell peers onto the stage. 'Tybalt's just knifing Mercutio.'

'Oh, we've been wasting our time. We are on again soon Heminges,' I say, searching for my hat and veil.

'We only need a little more of the balcony scene. Between that and what Condell has scribbled, and whatever's left of Will's copies, we'll have a good chunk to make our claim with the Stationers' Guild,' Heminges says.

'What claim?' I ask.

'We'll have to move quickly on to the rest of Will's plays,' Heminges says, then comes right to my ear to add: 'All the words must go to a printer, and now, if Burbage's state is what it seems. Every printer in London would be happy to get his hands on the complete works of William Shakespeare, we could command a top price.'

'Wait until we come off, and I'll assist you with Master Burbage. He needs a soft touch,' I say.

'We have time yet. Get Burbage up and get him remembering,' Heminges says, returning to his basket balcony.

'Remind Master Heminges that there are penalties for players who are late for their cues,' I say to Condell.

He looks to Heminges, his clown face dead-pan: 'You heard him.'

But I have more: 'Inform him that Nicholas Tooley, shareholder of the King's Men, will make application for ten years' unpaid shares, if he comes off to find that Master Heminges has taken steps in his grand plan to force any more words out of Master Burbage.'

As I disappear up the stairs, Heminges shouts bitterly after me: 'I knew you'd come back because you wanted something!'

IT is 2006 and I have just been cast in a production of Robert Bolt's *A Man for All Seasons* in the city, a short walk from my new home, a terrace house in Pyrmont, just across Darling Harbour from the theatre.

I'll be playing Richard Rich, the villain of the piece. I love a chance to play the villain because it's far more interesting exploring ways to be hated by a crowd.

With rehearsals just ahead and my new day job producing commercials and corporate videos, I know I won't have much time to write, which makes me all the more determined to finish the second draft of act one of *Merely Players*.

Life feels more stable than it has for months, and I am

sitting in my sunny spare room at Jono's computer. I dig out the compact disc I saved the file onto in the weeks after his death almost two years before, not knowing when I'd have the time and headspace to complete the work.

But the file icon looks different when it loads. I double click on it and wait while it takes its time to open.

Eventually, the word processor spits out a version of the file's contents. It's there, but it needs plenty of formatting.

So I start applying myself in the evenings after work, and at the weekends, when I have no place to be and no-one to be accountable to.

Despite the visitation of death, and probably because of it, I am still driven by the need to tell stories, seeking solace in the painful places that make for great drama.

I no longer see any reason to put up barriers between my life and the lives of these players. Act One steers itself to its inevitable conclusion: the death of Richard Burbage, the shining light of the Globe playhouse, on the rehearsal room floor.

Wise saws and modern instances

AS WE DESCEND the stairs from the stage, Heminges is at my heels like a dog wanting a morsel.

'None would believe it's ten years since you were on the stage, Tooley, you played that very well,' he says. I feel his hands trying to catch my arm, but I pull ahead of him.

As my eyes grow accustomed to the darkness, I can see nothing.

'Where is Master Burbage? It's nearly time for him to go on,' I say, seeking him.

'Burbage?' Heminges mutters. 'Aye, Condell, you saw him last, where is Burbage?'

'Don't make me say it,' Condell says, his white face floating in the black.

'Say what?' I ask.

'He's had a little... spill,' Condell adds.

'What?'

Condell mutters, turning to me. 'They were going at each other, he was going at Burbage, and...'

I speak over him: 'Oh, was he?'

'Aye, wanting Burbage to remember the play,' Condell adds.

'Where is Master Burbage now?' I ask, and I sense the blade of fear in my voice.

'I have to go on,' Condell says, turning away.

'Where is he?' I cry.

Condell points to the pile of papers that is now becoming visible in the lines of light. The plays I had in their piles have blood smeared across them, with large droplets running to the floor, where the earth is soaking up a great pool of red beneath a mess of paper.

ACTING LIKE SHAKESPEARE REALLY MATTERS

As I take it in, Condell scuttles, escaping up the steps.

Then I see the feet, my Master's feet, sticking out of the page pile.

'Let's get you into your chair Master Burbage,' I say, with a Fool's hope.

The feet do not move. Nothing about the paper moves, apart from the streamlets of blood. About where my Master's head should be, I pull at the mess to get to him. Underneath, I see his skin in the shadows, his swarthy face paint smeared with traces of red.

'What have you done?'

'I was only trying to get him to see sense,' Heminges says, suddenly at my side. 'He wouldn't remember his lines.'

'But there is so much blood,' I say, pulling at more of the papers.

'I did not mean to knock him,' Heminges says, drawing away from what we have found.

'Knock him? Knock him with what?'

'I meant shake him... I didn't mean to shake him.'

'You shook him? A frail old man, and you shook him?' I ask.

'He just fell over. I didn't mean for him to die.'

I don't want to say it, but I do: 'He's supposed to play the Apothecary, and soon.'

Heminges draws further away. I prepare to get in his way if he makes for the stairs.

'You were hoping to stop the play,' I say.

'Not like this.'

'I know you to be a man who likes to see his will done, Heminges, but this is a dark path to getting your way.'

'Nay, think not that of me Tooley. I did not mean to kill him, I swear it,' he says.

My eyes have fully adjusted now, and as I pull the

papers away from my Master, his head jiggles, lifeless.

'Dear God, think of what we'll have to say to Mrs Burbage! She will not bear this... oh Dickie, not like this,' I say, falling to my knees.

'We could just say he keeled over,' Heminges offers.

'You will tell her the truth!'

'Such an old man should not spend his days around the playhouse.'

'I should never have left. This would never have happened if I hadn't left,' I say.

'Don't blame yourself, Tooley, he was on his last legs.'

I get to my feet with the anger. 'I don't blame myself, it is just the latest tragedy in the management of this playhouse by Master John Heminges, who never listens to the other men, and must always see his will done!'

'Manager of the King's Men? Me? Oh duckie, our manager lies dead before you. Burbage never let me manage anything,' Heminges says, wiping the sweat from his temples.

'You always tried your best to undermine him, and you managed to get rid of me.'

'You left, I never pushed you.'

'I was Master Burbage's apprentice. I could have managed him, and I could have managed this playhouse better than you,' I say, and I know it is heresy.

'So you're back to claim your rightful place, is that it?' Heminges asks.

The groaning of the beams draws my attention to the play upstairs.

'Help me get his costume off,' I say.

'What?'

'Get the cloak, and the hat. You're going on as the Apothecary,' I tell Heminges.

'I don't know the lines.'

'They're inside the cloak,' I say.

We lift my Master and some of the pages stick to his face. The cloak is fastened at his neck, and as I undo it, his body collapses and Heminges lets him fall.

'Be careful!' I say.

'Well, he can't feel it,' Heminges says.

We pull the cloak away, and the pages pinned inside come with it.

'How long has he been reading his lines from his armpits?' Heminges asks.

'Take the hat, and get ready,' I say.

'Where are we up to?' he asks, throwing the bloody cloak around himself.

From the third step, I look to the stage.

'There is still some time,' I say.

'Tooley. You must not think ill of me,' he says.

'It does not matter what I think of you.'

I start helping the unwieldy cloak to fall properly around Heminges, and I am about to remind him to take the hat, when a sound on the stairs signals Condell's return.

'Are we going on?' Condell says.

'Of course we are going on. Heminges will play the Apothecary,' I say.

Heminges shows the pages inside his cloak. 'I've got the lines.'

'He's on soon, very soon,' Condell says.

'I know,' Heminges says, testing if he can see the lines inside the cloak.

'Tell me what happened,' I ask Condell. 'Heminges told me he knocked Burbage.'

'I didn't knock him, he knocked his head when he fell,' Heminges complains.

'Because you shook him,' I say, to silence Heminges.

'Is that what happened?' I ask Condell.

Condell shrugs: 'I was watching the stage, scribing the play.'

I have them both under my gaze. 'If you'd only waited for me to come off you could have had all the words you wanted.'

'It doesn't matter now, just wait until I come off before you tell anyone,' Heminges says.

'Now he wants to wait!' I say, loudly.

'So I can make a proper account of what happened.'

'Aye, perchance old Burbage's time was just up?' Condell says.

I feel them starting to square their story. 'He should not have gone this way. He should have gone to his grave from his own bed,' I say.

'He was ailing ever since the winter,' Heminges says.

Just then, the papers near Burbage's head flutter. His feet move and he coughs.

IT is later in 2006 and I am sitting in the café where my new partner Richard is the chef. A week before, I'd been down with a terribly sore throat for days, and I woke late, feeling as though I'd slept very deeply.

In my stupor, I realised I was due to meet a friend in less than half an hour, showered lightning fast, jumped in the car, and as I looked in the rear vision mirror to reverse out the driveway, I noticed my reflection looked weird.

It felt perhaps that my face was still asleep, so I gave myself a gentle slap.

At the bathroom mirror, the truth revealed itself subtly: the whole right-hand side of my face was slumped, including my eyelid. I could feel the muscles trying to lift internally, but nothing was happening on the surface.

I called my friend and said I'd have to cancel, then went back to bed, thinking that by the time I woke up, all would be well.

But it wasn't. I had woken up with a case of Bell's Palsy.

At the hospital, the first of many practitioners failed to look at my face. I was prescribed a course of steroids, and told things might get better after a few weeks.

I went to my doctor and he looked up his notes on this condition, which has been afflicting people with varying states of permanency for millennia, yet he didn't once look at my face.

I went to see an acupuncturist, who assured me that his modality has been getting faces moving forever, yet throughout two weeks of treatments, he failed to look at the problem. After I caught him giving me a strange glance when he thought I wasn't looking, I didn't go back.

A fallen face is an aberration, apparently.

At the grocery shop, the shop assistant slowed down her speech, obviously thinking I was stupid.

At the takeaway shop, an old acquaintance either didn't recognise me, or did but fled in shock.

A good friend looked pained by my sunken features, especially my difficulty with speaking, and just nodded, concerned yet remote.

Without my usual speed, or courage, of response, I stopped going out of the house.

And after a few weeks of that cold nerve pain coursing through my head and shoulders, I wondered if this was going to be my new life from now on.

Worst of all, I'd only recently started a new

relationship, and presenting with a permanent facial disfiguration was not an ideal prospect.

It wasn't until a friend of a friend heard about my Bell's Palsy that a solution reared its 'ugly head'. She'd had Bell's Palsy herself, and her advice was simple and a little shocking: 'If you want your face back, change your life.'

My great new job was only six months old. My dawning relationship even younger.

These were not circumstances I wanted to change, but a fortnight of being treated like the village idiot or a special needs case weighed heavily on me.

I decided the relationship was not up for negotiation. The job, however, was, so I resigned, and got myself to a naturopath.

She was the first practitioner to look me in the eye, name my condition out loud without fear, and tell me with surety she knew she could fix me. Prescribing higher than usual doses of omega-3 oil and vitamin B, she got to the essence of the cause of many Bell's Palsy cases – strangulated nerves.

Our facial nerves emerge from the brain via a small hole in the skull near each ear, and if something – in my case a virus – causes swelling in the region, the nerves can get pinched and simply shut down.

Much of the condition's nature remains a mystery, especially the reason some people recover fully, some partially, and some (the minority) never, but advice from someone who'd been there was all I had to go on.

At the café, I am waiting for Richard – known to everyone as Dickie – to take a short break. I will ask if he'll open his house to me now that my income has suddenly diminished. His open heart tells me that he is just as interested in what lies under my surface. I have taken courage that work will come my way at the right time, and have focused on eating well and resting.

The Bell's Palsy came just a few short weeks after I finished the long run of *A Man for All Seasons* and I am amazed at the proximity of this affliction to the time when I was presenting my face nightly on the stage. I don't realise it in that moment, but this fear will contribute to me not performing for the next ten years.

'DICKIE?' I say, pushing past Heminges to get to him.

'Where are we up to?' my Master says.

'Oh, Dickie,' I say, cleaning the blood from his mouth. 'Help me get him up,' I say to Heminges.

'Am I on yet?' Burbage says, stopping us.

'You've had a fall,' I say, taking his head between my hands and seeking his eyes.

'Who are you?' my Master asks me.

'It is I, Tooley.'

'Tooley? Nay, Tooley is a boy, not an old lady,' he says.

'Nick, I am your Nick, who was your apprentice,' I say, as he blinks back at me.

'Nay, my Nick Tooley left the playhouse many years ago,' he says, then, pointing at Heminges: 'Who's that one?'

'That is Master Heminges,' I say.

'Heminges? Nay, this crag of a face cannot be young Master Heminges. Am I on yet?' my Master says.

I look to the other men, then back at my Master, who wears the innocence of a boy.

'Just rest yourself for a moment,' Condell says, weakly.

Master Burbage points at him: 'Who is that one?'

'It is Henry Condell, just come from the stage,' I say.

Condell's face is broad with wonder: 'Heaven and hell! Burbage, we thought you were dead,' he says.

'I am perfectly well,' my Master says.

'Were you playing with me?' Condell asks.

'Playing?' my Master asks.

Now Condell is angry: 'Aye, were you playing dead with me?'

Before an answer comes, Heminges draws me and Condell aside.

'He is too frail to do it, I'll go on,' Heminges says quickly.

'He was dead when you left for the stage,' Condell says.

'He's not that frail, he can do it himself,' I say.

'Just now you were saying he's a "poor, frail old man!",' Heminges says, right in my face.

'You shook him, and he fell, and he was out cold!' Condell says.

'Luckily for you he's made of sterner stuff than we knew,' I tell Heminges.

'If he goes up there and swoons again it will not be my fault,' he responds.

'You'd best get him ready, he's on very soon,' Condell warns, looking at the stage from the third step.

'We know!' Heminges and I say at the same time.

'I cannot lie here talking to a washer woman and old men, I must ready myself,' my Master says, trying to get himself upright.

I notice the beams groaning. 'Go up and tell them to pad it out,' I shout at Condell, who nods and disappears into the light.

My Master is dragging himself upwards on Heminges, who notices something in the shadows.

ACTING LIKE SHAKESPEARE REALLY MATTERS

'This is where all the blood is from,' Heminges says, holding up the familiar bottle.

'It's pig's blood, fresh from the tannery by the river,' Master Burbage says.

'Aha, only pig's blood?' Heminges says, relieved.

'Aye, they save me the best for my make-up,' my Master says.

We help him to his chair, kicking the papers out of the way.

'You took a little tumble, is all. You must have knocked over the bottle Tooley was using to write with,' Heminges says, laughing. 'That's it, that's what happened.'

'Why were you writing with my bottle of pig's blood? You'll have to pay me for it,' my Master says.

'You'll have to ask Master Heminges that later,' I say. 'We've got to get you ready.'

Heminges has started collecting the pages of play at our feet, and I usher him well out of the way, then, under my breath, I address him, forcing him against the wall beside the steps.

'If you meant to stop this play by rendering Master Burbage incapable, then I am happy to report you will fail. Left to his own devices, he might be artless, but in the company of other players, my Master will come to life yet,' I say.

'Who am I?' Master Burbage says, breaking my hard stare into Heminges' artful eyes.

'You are Richard Burbage, player of...' I say, until he interrupts.

'I know that woman, who am I playing? Am I the Moor? Or am I King Richard?' Master Burbage says.

'You are the Apothecary,' I say, richly.

'The Apothecary? I don't recall a play about an

Apothecary. Aha, Master Shakespeare has written me a new one!'

'Nay...' Heminges manages, before I cut him off.

'Aye, Master Shakespeare has written us a new play, "The Apothecary of Mantua",' I say.

'Am I a wealthy man?' Master Burbage asks.

'You are a great man of business, who visits the city of Verona,' I say, encouraging Heminges out of the cloak and hat.

'Ah, Verona, and I have an adventure there?' my Master asks.

'Aye, a young man is coming to ask you for a draught of poison,' I say.

'Aha, there's always a draught of poison in an adventure, but I won't give it over without some money from the lad.'

'Good, Master Burbage, you know your part,' I say, as Condell returns.

'There is time, they will wait for him,' he says.

'Can a knock to the head restore so much to an old man?' Heminges asks, close to my ear.

'He might have been like this for years, and you would not have known it, for he's just been taking his cues from the rest of you,' I say.

'You think we did not notice a completely addled man, living amongst us?' Heminges asks.

'Living and working, cheek by jowl with you all, and you fools had no inkling,' I reply.

'I confess I did not see it. He's a clever old bird,' Condell says, returning to his chair.

'I lived with many such people in the nunnery. Sometimes they need words more than they need food, but just a little goes a very long way.'

I approach my Master cautiously, signalling at

ACTING LIKE SHAKESPEARE REALLY MATTERS

Heminges to hand over the Apothecary's cloak and hat.

'Master Burbage, the Apothecary is on soon. You only need your cloak and hat,' I say, making a great show of putting the hat on, as though it was a crown. 'You are the greatest Apothecary in Italy.'

'Aye, and the whole story hinges on what potion I give to the hero,' my Master says.

'The noble Apothecary,' I venture.

'What if they see that I am not what I say I am?' he asks, faltering.

'When did Master Burbage become such a mewling kitten?' I ask, helping him to stand and letting me put him inside the cloak.

'But if I forget?'

'You forget,' I say, 'and if Richard Burbage forgets, he sits, and he is Burbage, and they watch, and they listen, and he finds his way back, and then he remembers. You are Richard Burbage, player of the Lord Chamberlain's Men.'

'I am Richard Burbage, player,' he says.

I check the stage from the third stair. 'Come, it is time.'

My master stands to his full height, breathes in, and leads the way up the stairs.

IT is 2007 and I am sitting in the quietude of the State Library in Sydney, downstairs in the reading room, where I have spent the morning analysing the only known primary sources about the King's Men, the first performers of Shakespeare's work.

There is not much left to shed a clear light on these men and the world they inhabited – court documents, primarily, but scant literary or dramatic paperwork.

So I am surprised and delighted to find their wills, which provide some of the most detailed information, securing as they did the inheritance of playhouse shares.

Nicholas Tooley's stands out from those of Heminges, Burbage and Condell in that it has an abundance of instructions about monies to be given to the women in his life, which includes the wives, sisters and daughters of the extended Burbage family.

The manner in which Tooley worded these bequests hints at the kind of man he was:

> *'I doe giue unto vnto her daughter Elizabethe Burbadge als Maxey the summe of tenn pounds to be paied vnto her owne proper hands (therwithall to buy she such things as she shall thincke most meete to weare in remembrance of mee...)'*

I get a sense of an unmarried man who was well acquainted with the social manners of female friendship, and these womens' legal needs in his absence. For Elizabeth, and other Burbage women, he added:

> *'And my will is that an acquitance vnder her onlie hand and seale, shalbe a sufficient dischange in Lawe to my executors for paiement thereof to all intents purposes and construccons and as fullie as if her pretend husband should make and seale the same with her'*

I think it is clear Tooley was telling his executors, Cuthbert Burbage and Henry Condell, that of the long list of women whose debts he forgave and what sums they were to be in receipt of, not a penny was to go to any husband, real, potential or construed.

Tooley also made tender mention of the woman who took 'motherlie care over mee' – Mrs Elizabeth Burbage senior, sister-in-law of Richard Burbage – 'in whose howse I do now lodge.'

Tooley's will reveals that he used two names, but he calls his birth name an 'alias'. He also seems like a man

ACTING LIKE SHAKESPEARE REALLY MATTERS

who enjoyed talking about clothing. Whatever Elizabeth, her female relatives, and the man known as Nicholas Wilkinson shared over fashion or accessories that were 'meete to weare' was perhaps done with a level of fun.

A man who'd played a woman, who spent time being perceived as a woman in the Elizabethan and Jacobean era, could have made such specific references because the Burbage women were a coterie who enjoyed the company of same sex-attracted men. They sound to me like Nicholas Wilkinson's fag hags.

Academia has rarely countenanced the possibility, despite gay men and transgender womens' strong tradition of driving the performing arts.

We know some of plays Tooley appeared in, but there is a record of only one specific part, a minor male role in Webster's *The Duchess of Malfi*, very late in his life. The rest of his performances remain concealed behind an uncharacteristic lack of attribution.

These discoveries, with my emerging militancy about sexual diversity, my sensibility for women, and my gut feeling, tell me that Nicholas Wilkinson, alias Nicholas Tooley, is a candidate for one of the mystery men who played the female parts of William Shakespeare.

It is the last piece of surety I need to embark on my latest draft of *Merely Players*.

Filled with inspiration, in the afternoon I go upstairs into the older wing of the library, The Mitchell Collection, where I see a first edition of Shakespeare's First Folio displayed in a glass cabinet.

Only two hundred and thirty-three folios remain of the original print run. This is Sydney's only copy.

Daily, the library staff open it to a new page. The occasion I see this folio, it shows a scene from *A Midsummer Night's Dream* which includes the lines I played

as a petulant, long-suffering perfectionist Peter Quince:
> *"'Ninus' tomb," man: why, you must not speak that yet; that you answer to Pyramus: you speak all your part at once, cues and all. Pyramus enter: your cue is past; it is, 'never tire'.'*

MY Master has command of himself as the Apothecary, but I am not content to stay by the stage, I want to see the faces of Heminges and Condell.

As I reach the corner of the steps, I pause and listen for their mutterings.

Condell is laughing. 'You have forgotten what it is to play. No player ever knows what will come out of his mouth when he walks onto the stage, you know that. If Burbage reads only half his lines, he makes up the other half of the illusion with all his hot air! Oh, I am filled with delight at the idea. We could go on playing until we're worse than Burbage is now, you and I.'

'I may have to, Condell,' I hear Heminges reply. 'I'll never play a new part, not now. I don't have Burbage's courage. What use is an old player who cannot read his lines?'

'We'll con your lines together, you and I. We don't have to tell anyone upstairs,' Condell says.

But Heminges is not satisfied. 'Will you stand by my side when I am so blind I am about to fall off the stage, and cannot find my own way off?'

'We can count the number of paces from the back of the stage to the front,' Condell suggests.

'Every day I see less,' Heminges says, on a whisper.

'I know it, the work you did on Burbage's face was not always the best lately,' Condell says, and I can hear in his voice that he is trying to work his foolery.

ACTING LIKE SHAKESPEARE REALLY MATTERS

'I wanted a book of Will's plays. All the university fellows would have been happy to pay for it. I wanted to hold that in my hand, and retire, without any of the younger men knowing about my eyes,' Heminges says, bitterly.

Silence, for a moment. I imagine Condell searching for a riposte. 'You should have told us you were thinking about your book again, instead of just landing it on us.'

'I wanted us to have enough coin to stay warm by our fires instead of playing until we go like Burbage,' Heminges says, his voice dropping to its lowest.

'Steady on, we're not as bad as Burbage, unless there's something you're not telling me?' Condell says, his arms starting to dance. 'You'd tell me if I was, wouldn't you?'

'If I could just see the words, I could do the whole thing myself, but even by the light of day my eyes are failing me,' Heminges says.

'Come now,' Condell laughs, 'how many plays did Will Shakespeare write?'

'More than thirty.'

'Perchance almost forty. We'll just have to remember the bits that are missing, and write them down,' Condell says, starting to play with the papers.

'We are all heading for our graves Condell, we don't have enough time to remember.'

'Nay, remembering roles is nothing. You won't need your eyes to remember any of yours. What we have in our heads was graven into our skulls. All of it, drilled every night so that any play might be called the next day. I barely remember my prayers, Heminges, but I remember every one of my lines! Did you not start out playing the hero's best friends? Then they moved you up to the gallant nobles and lords, long before you started doing the idle and fussy fathers?'

'Aye, that's about the sum of it,' Heminges answers.

'They started me on the hero's second-best friends, then I went to the clowns, and the sophisticated Fools, and I always did the gravediggers, even when I was young. Burbage did all the heroes, of course. Hamlet, Othello, Richard, Lear, and Tooley did all the wives and maidens. Between us, we are the complete plays of Master Shakespeare!'

But Heminges is quick with the awful truth: 'Except Burbage has nothing in his receptacle,' he complains.

A noise comes from within the crowd, but Heminges and Condell don't seem to feel it yet.

Bur-bage, Bur-bage, Bur-bage!

'Then we'll sit down together and start from the beginning, like boys at school,' Condell says.

'Nay, Condell, you cannot clown me into it.'

'It's the job of a Fool to make men laugh, when all they want to do is cry.'

IT is 2007 and Richard and I are living in a fibro cottage in north Leura. We haven't renovated the house yet, but we've made a great start on the half-acre of European-style gardens, with drystone walls and thousands of bulbs pushing their heads up as the winter begins to lose its bite.

The security of living in a family unit again after all the angst and upheaval of the past two years has meant I have finally finished writing the second draft of *Merely Players*.

I have Jono's computer perched on the end of an old teak dressing table in the hallway by the front door. It's large enough for a very small office space.

ACTING LIKE SHAKESPEARE REALLY MATTERS

All the backstage humour Jono encouraged out of me is in there, the camaraderie and conflict of actors behind the scenes. This element of the play will remain, because I will fight for it across several rewrites to come. It is what I love the most about my idea: two actors, friends and rivals, with something to take care of backstage, while the show itself is taking place.

Later, warmed to the bone by the embers of the open fire we sometimes light on the bush block behind house in the winter, I acknowledge this milestone to myself.

Despite the odds of it never happening, I have a whole, imperfect draft of my play. For the only time in its life, *Merely Players* has scenes in Stratford-upon-Avon and London; several members of Shakespeare's family fighting for a share in his legacy; printers and stationers, and England's Master of the Revels all make an appearance in the story of how Shakespeare's First Folio came into being out of the mess left when William Shakespeare died. The play requires a cast of thirty characters played by eight actors.

I know it needs plenty of work, and that offering it to an industry that barely stages work on the scale of *Nicholas Nickleby* or *Amadeus* these days is probably madness, but it exists.

Alone by the fire, I let the heat of the logs sear the self recognition into me. It has taken me four years, and much loss, but at last I feel a sense of creative power again.

THE noise rumbles through the wooden frame around us.

Bur-bage, Bur-bage, Bur-bage!

I think to announce my presence, but Master Condell

gives a low chuckle, and I keep listening.

'He'll be drinking up the admiration,' he says.

'Aye, he never forgets to go for another call, have you noticed!' Heminges says, planted on a stool like a boy.

'It is more than admiration,' I say. 'It is love.'

'How long have you been standing there?' Heminges asks.

I ignore the question, and say, to Condell: 'You forgot about the queens.'

'The queens?' Condell asks.

'I also played all the queens,' I say.

'Aye, that's true enough,' he says.

'Tooley, forget what you think you heard,' Heminges says.

Still, I ignore him. 'Burbage is coming, just make as though it's the old days. We are the Lord Chamberlain's Men now, remember?' I say.

'Would that I cut the figure I did in the old days,' Condell says, stopping and posing before me.

'Suck it in, just like the rest of us!' I say. 'Elizabeth sits on the throne, and Lear is not yet written.'

'If it really is the old days, we are running the playhouse, then it's the complete fantasy,' Heminges says from his stool.

'Just play it, and I'll try to draw him back to us from there,' I say, my Master's shadow already cast across the stairs.

'Out of the way woman!' he says, handing me his cloak and making for the privy. 'Good crowd, again,' he says, seeking some response from us.

'You had them in your hands today,' I say, trying to move the other men from their silence.

'Fine work, Burbage,' Condell offers from his corner.

'Aye, very fine,' Heminges mutters.

ACTING LIKE SHAKESPEARE REALLY MATTERS

'The crowd knows a good play when it's shown one,' Burbage says, shaking off the praise.

'But it was you they loved the most,' I say to his back.

Yet it's as though I have said nothing.

'I never seem to piss out as much as it feels I should,' he groans, finishing off. 'I need a drink,' he says as he emerges.

'Aye, Master Burbage,' I say.

'Pour one for all the men,' he orders.

Master Condell fills a round of cups and hand them to every man.

'Don't give drinks to the washer woman, it will only look bad for her,' my Master says.

I nod to Condell and step back as Master Burbage raises a toast: 'To tomorrow's plays.'

Condell and Heminges give their assent: 'Tomorrow's plays.'

My Master downs his drink in one. 'Leave me now,' he says to the other men.

They do not move, so I usher Heminges and Condell up the stairs.

'You tried getting the words out of Burbage your way, Heminges,' I whisper. 'Both of you, leave us, and let me try mine.'

They take their cups and leave. While I wait for them to disappear, I collect the last of the costumes from the floor.

'Woman, have they said what plays we're doing tomorrow?' my Master asks, hovering over his table.

'Nay, Master Burbage.'

'Go and ask Master Shakespeare, and I'll give you a coin, lass,' he says.

'Aye,' I say, and retreat into the shadows. If he believes himself to be truly alone, I am sure this is the

MERELY PLAYERS

moment my Master will reveal his secret.

He sits, listens for noises on the stairs, and when he hears none, I see him draw a key from around his neck, which he fits into a small box underneath his table. From inside, he draws out various small papers, laying them out carefully, reading bits and pieces, laughing at some, quoting others.

I must judge my moment carefully and give my Master enough time, so I clear my throat and return to his side. He throws his hat over the open box and the papers.

'Dickie, come, it is time to prepare for tomorrow's plays,' I say.

'Is there anyone about?' he asks.

'Nay, they're off counting the money,' I say.

Just when I think he has truly forgotten the old days, he reaches for me.

'Give us a kiss first.'

I dodge him. 'Nay, Master Shakespeare said we'll be starting with one of our old favourites. Can you guess?'

'The one about the plucky little legal lass?' Master Burbage asks.

'Nay, more favoured than Portia,' I say.

'More favoured than Portia? I liked her well enough. Who did I like better than her?'

I have made sure to be standing in a sliver of light, and I start to act:

'Deny thy father and refuse thy name;
Or, if thou wilt not, be but sworn my love,
And I'll no longer be a Capulet.'

'Juliet!' Master Burbage shouts.

'Aye. Come, we'll run your lines from the death scene,' I say, pulling at the basket Master Heminges made into our balcony. 'You, Romeo, enter the chapel of the Capulets, and, I, Juliet, am lying here.'

'Dead.'

'Nay, I am not dead, I only sleep, but to you, it is as though I am dead,' I say. 'From "Ah, dear Juliet, why art thou yet so fair?",' and I lie myself down as though on a cold slab.

My Master takes his cue without pause:
'Shall I believe
That unsubstantial death is amorous,
And that...'

'Don't tell me, I know it,' he says, not pausing.
'Shall I believe
That unsubstantial death is amorous,
And that...'

Despite the silence, I can do nothing for my Master. I lie still, and hear him shuffling over to the papers. If I am correct, he will find what he needs among them.

'Dickie?' I whisper, when I can hold it in no longer.

'Wait! Stay there Juliet, you sleep!' he hisses.

Soon he shuffles back to my side, and I feel one hand gently travel across my eyes, holding them closed as he speaks. The other clutches the pages I feel brushing across my front.

'Ay me, sweet Juliet,
Are thy still so fair? Do I believe
That death loves thee too much...'

And in that moment I know all that he has done. All that the papers in the cloak mean, hidden and read as needed. I draw his hand away and look up into his eyes, and at the same time I take the pages from his other hand and let them fall onto the mess at the foot of our slab.

'You do not need this printer's rubbish, Dickie. Let it go.'

'I knew the lines once, I knew them all,' he says.

'We still know them all, my love,' I say, and both my hands go to the sides of his pained face, as we speak the lines together:

> *Ah, dear Juliet,*
> *Why art thou yet so fair? Shall I believe*
> *That unsubstantial death is amorous,*
> *And that the lean abhorred monster keeps*
> *Thee here in dark to be his paramour?'*

Now, I fold myself against him, and his arms come up to catch me. Though it will look as if I am dead, my head rests against his shoulder, right by his ear, and I whisper the lines into his receptacle as he speaks them:

> *'For fear of that, I still will stay with thee;*
> *And never from this palace of dim night*
> *Depart again: here, here will I remain*
> *With worms that are thy chamber-maids; O, here*
> *Will I set up my everlasting rest,*
> *And shake the yoke of inauspicious stars*
> *From this world-wearied flesh. Eyes, look your last!*
> *Arms, take your last embrace! And, lips, O you*
> *The doors of breath, seal with a righteous kiss*
> *A dateless bargain to engrossing death!'*

And my mouth is as full with his kiss as his is with the words.

'You know my lines better than I do, woman,' he says when we part, his look as tender as it ever was.

'The last time we did that was before the Queen,' I say. 'I could see her from my tomb, for her dress it was all dandied-up with little jewels, and in the light of the candles they did flicker. But in the darkness where her face should be, two watery jewels hung for her eyes, and I knew then that good Queen Bess had known love the way Juliet had known it, the way I had known it, at least once before she went to her grave, God rest her soul.'

'Good Queen Bess, she is gone to her grave?' Dickie asks.

'Oh... nay, Dickie,' I say, but it is too late to take the words back.

'Do they laugh when it's a comedy, or do they laugh when it's a tragedy?' my Master asks, struggling.

'Come, more of *Romeo and Juliet*, sit by me,' I venture, but he is back at his box.

'My Juliet promised she would always be there, when I came off the stage, but she lied,' he says, fingers finding truths inside that box that I dare not know.

'Perchance she had to go?' I ask.

'I never released her,' he replies.

'But you did not come after her. She was past the age of an apprentice, well past. There was nothing more for her to play, and she could not stay and play your wife any longer.'

'It was she who sent me to the printers,' he says, looking over words on the page.

'She? How?'

'I didn't need any of this until she left me,' my Master says, and I think he is only sitting back in his chair, but he drops the box and the contents spill. 'I heard it said, you see, that a printer would be a very good friend to an old player. The printers said they could put all my words together in one place, on these cunning little pages where they could never be forgotten. King Richard I gave to printer Thomas Creede. Thomas Pavier, he took King Lear off my mind, and Richard Smethwick, he got my prizes... Hamlet and Romeo. But they lied to me too. Always cutting, always changing... they were never word-perfect.'

'Rest now Dickie,' I say, though I know he never will.

MERELY PLAYERS

'I think she is gone, our Queen, and I think we are not playing this play tomorrow. I told Mrs Burbage I would be home tonight. I must take all these papers home to keep her warm.'

This strange eventful history

IT IS 2008 and I am sitting with a group of actors in the living room of a holiday house. It is already late and yet the first reading of *Merely Players* has entered its third hour. I'm enjoying the process, but I have misgauged the length of the play, and there are at least fifteen pages to get through. People are being patient, although it's a weeknight and many have to be at work in the morning.

This play-reading group of actors meets regularly to lift new plays off the page. It's the first time in my life I have been part of anything like this, and it has been a night of great highs and lows.

My play is a heaving mass of too many ideas. 'Rich' and 'detailed' will be the kind phrases used to describe it. *Far too bloody long and over-stuffed* is my immediate sense about fifteen minutes in.

Mistress Wilkinson, alias Nicholas Tooley, is being read by a woman. When I'd asked this actress to forgive me for thinking she was just right to read the role of a man, she laughed and said it was not the first time.

The only piece of advice I gave her was to underline that Tooley is a woman simply because he knows himself to be one. I will realise in years to come that I should just have just altered the pronouns and said *she* is a woman, simply because *she* knows herself to be one. It's a subtle but powerful difference.

For now, my husband Richard is showing his delight at a powerful monologue.

> *'A woman moved is like a fountain troubled,*
> *Muddy, ill-seeming, thick, bereft of beauty,*
> *And while it is so, none so dry or thirsty*
> *Will deign to sip or touch one drop of it.'*

He leans across to attract my attention, points to the actress speaking the lines, and mouths: *Did you write that?*

No, I mouth back, *that's Shakespeare.*

I still have plenty of work to do.

BEFORE I can form words to comfort my Master, a figure pushes past me and dives for the box on the floor, where the hidden papers have all fallen into Will's pages.

'How much did the printers pay you, Burbage?' Heminges says with his unmistakable fire.

I let out a cry and cover that part of my chest where my Master had kissed me, but he only turns to his table as though he were getting ready for the stage, and starts to sing:

'Romeo! Romeo! Wherefore are thou roaming now?
Tell thy father and give up thy name;
Or alone alas I will remain.'

The words have none of their former amusement. Only a brittle, old man, singing for understanding.

'Why didn't you just give Will's copies to the printers?' Heminges asks.

'Will's copies?' my Master says, not turning, but laughing. 'They were never Will's copies! A playwright never owns the copies, he only writes a play down, in handwriting no player could ever read, and he sells his foul scribblings to the playhouse. When a player has conned his lines, he can do whatever he likes with the papers.'

'When we are gone, where is the play then?' Heminges says, leaning over Master Burbage. 'It will not hang in the air of a playhouse, it cannot be drawn down by another player.'

My Master shrugs, and smiles thinly back at

ACTING LIKE SHAKESPEARE REALLY MATTERS

Heminges. 'When we are gone, so too will the plays be gone. That is the way it has been since long before we walked the stage, and that is the way it will be long after we are all in our graves.'

'Burbage...' Heminges says, but my Master cuts him off.

'Silence! No player will ever own my parts. He might play Romeo right now, that leggy player, but it is my part, mine! He is only borrowing it. He is only parroting me.'

'But what of Master Shakespeare?' Heminges asks, not retreating.

My Master turns back to his preparations. 'When we are gone, none will have further need of him,' he says.

Then, in a deft move that takes me by surprise, he stands, pulls his bloodied doublet down straight, brushes his hand gently across my cheek, winks, and disappears up the stairs.

The beams above groan over we who are left, standing silently in a sea of papers.

Master Heminges moves first, his hands finding their way through the contents of my Master's box.

'How many of Burbage's roles do you know?' he asks me.

'All. We drilled them enough.'

'Every one?' he demands.

'You know the job of an apprentice as well as I: copy the lines for your Master, from the playwright's pages, and cue him when he forgets,' I say.

'Aye, we all of us did it,' Condell says quietly from his corner, 'but to have remembered all of Burbage's, and all your own, that is the task of a lifetime.'

'There were too many lines for one man to hold by himself, so I just kept up the remembering,' I say.

'Why did you not say so before?' Heminges says, his voice breaking with hurt that raises an anger in me for its foolishness.

'Because it would have shown Master Burbage up!' I say. 'Sometimes it is wiser to make believe, for the sake of another man. That is something you could have tried long ago, Heminges.'

Heminges snorts, not looking at me, but still searching through the box. 'Every printed play is here, but none of it is as Shakespeare wrote it. Quickly, gather Will's copies together, and we'll put them back together. I'll take it all to the Stationers', now, before the printer's boys are finished their scribbling.'

Condell does not move, and when I do, it is not to help Heminges with his rat's work, it is back to where my basket still sits at the foot of the steps. I will have my things together in a moment and be up the stairs and gone before anyone notices.

But Condell is looking at me when I raise my eyes. He moves fast over to Heminges' side, and his white face is as open as a Fool's can be.

'I can see it now, this book,' he says.

'Oh, it'll be bigger than a book, more like a folio,' Heminges says, not looking up.

'A fo-l-io?' Condell says, spelling out the word by curling his mouth.

'It would be wise to set the price at a neat pound,' Heminges says, making his first pile of papers on the floor.

'A bargain, considering the cost,' Condell says.

'Oh, by the time they've set the type and paid for all the inks, there won't be too much change from a pound,' Heminges says, turning his back to the clown again and starting on another pile of papers.

ACTING LIKE SHAKESPEARE REALLY MATTERS

'Aye, the material costs will be great,' Condell says, dancing to the other side of Heminges.

'Well, what other costs will there be?' Heminges snorts.

'Oh, I think there is a cost, if you think about it,' Condell says, standing to his full height.

Heminges finally looks at him. 'Think about what?'

Condell locks eyes on me, and says: 'Make sure you have all the words first, especially the missing ones.'

Master Heminges follows Condell's gaze to me, sighs, puts the papers down, and comes to my side.

'Where are you going, Master Tooley? There is our curtain call yet, and you've earned it! Where are we up to?'

I cannot help it. I am close to the third step anyway, so I check.

'I missed the death scene,' I say. Never in my time in the playhouse have I ever missed a cue, but in my heart I feel nothing. 'There is not much left to play now, Heminges.'

When I check his face, he is still looking into me, saying nothing.

'How easily I slipped back into my old place in this playhouse, right at the bottom of the heap,' I say, standing taller than the both of them, on the third step. 'The fetcher, the one who picks the clothes up off the floor, and reminds all of you where the play is up to.'

'What you have, in your receptacle, it belongs to the King's Men, to all of us, and therefore so do you,' Condell says.

'It has been a very long time since I have belonged anywhere,' I say.

'Give us the words. It will not go unrewarded,' Heminges says.

His eyes carry a sympathy, but his mouth is set in a hard line. I decide to put that line to the test.

'Men like me, we are just a spectacle for the freak shows,' I say.

'Listen, these printed plays, they print players' names on them, do they not?' Heminges asks. 'We could add all our names to this folio. A man who has his name on a book of Shakespeare's plays could never be thought of as just a freak-show spectacle.'

'Shakespeare should go at the top of the page,' Condell says, picking up the thread.

'Then Burbage,' Heminges says.

'Then you, Heminges,' Condell adds.

'Only if such a position is warranted,' Heminges replies.

'Of course it is warranted,' Condell laughs.

'Well, you should go next,' Heminges says.

'Nay, I would not go on the list above my Master's name,' Condell says. 'All the masters must go first.'

'Alright, that's Phillips, and Pope, and Master Kempe. Then you, surely, at the top of the younger clowns,' Heminges offers.

'Only if you think I should go there,' Condell says, hands up like an innocent.

'Then the younger heroes. They'd best go in or they'll take it badly and run off to another playhouse,' Heminges says, ruefully.

'Put Lowin, and Cooke... but what of old Master Armin? Put him up there somewhere,' Condell says.

'Aye, if they're gone to their graves, and were shareholders, they must have a good position,' Heminges says. 'We'll have to make a proper account of all the men, but tomorrow.'

'What of all the women?' I ask, still on the third step.

ACTING LIKE SHAKESPEARE REALLY MATTERS

'What?' Heminges asks, noticing me again.

'You haven't mentioned anyone who played a woman.'

'Well, how many more words will that be?' Heminges asks.

'Oh, I have so many words in my head that a printer would have to sell his house to ink them, Master Heminges, but I would give them all, for only two words from you in return.'

'Two? Which two?' he asks, as though wanting to leap past me and stop me leaving.

'You can put my name on your book. I can do without Master Tooley now. I haven't needed him for many years. You can have him.'

Heminges is cautious. 'We might need to have two lists on the page, one on the left and one on the right.'

'Who goes at the top of the right-hand side?' Condell says, unable to help himself from making it a comic scene.

'That could flow on from the bottom of the left-hand side,' Heminges says.

'But if a player's name goes top right, but he's not a top player, we'll get complaints,' Condell warns, his eyes popping.

'I can see no other way to do it,' Heminges despairs.

'Have some of the King's Men done more than others?' I ask.

'It could be a matter of the number of parts played,' Heminges says.

'Master Shakespeare played but a few parts, and he's at the top of this list of yours,' I say. 'It seems to me you're putting all the skirt players at the bottom of the list, or nowhere.'

'Some of them were on the stage so little, just a queen

here or a maiden there. We cannot give the same place to boys as we give to men,' Heminges says, decided.

'We boys have long since grown into men, while your men have grown into dust. Remember all of us, or none,' I say.

Heminges turns his gaze away from me and back to the papers.

'I can see we are going to have to think on this, another time. I must get Will's copies to the Stationer. Where are we up to?' he asks.

I will not look.

'Let you not think on it too long, Master Heminges. If you want me to give you the contents of my receptacle, you'd best get in fast.'

'I can see you would keep your secrets,' Heminges says, stopping his pretend work.

'It is up to you, Master Heminges,' I say.

'Just like a woman!' he moans. 'Always it is up to a man to work out the ways of a woman! Would that you thought on this as a man would!'

'It was a woman who got the words for you,' I say, as calmly as Desdemona goes to her death.

'Which woman?' Heminges growls.

'It was Juliet who raised Romeo for you, right before your eyes.'

'And I suppose you and Burbage... it wasn't all an act, duckie?' Heminges says, mocking.

'I think we can guess the answer, Heminges,' Condell says, face stripped of humour.

'He rewarded me in ways that I needed, in ways that he found he needed,' I say.

'Can your base needs have been anything like love?' Heminges asks.

I cannot think what to say, so I quote, just as I did

when my Master called for a line. It is Lear that comes to my mind:

> *'O, reason not the need! Our basest beggars*
> *Are in the poorest thing superfluous.*
> *Allow not nature more than nature needs,*
> *Man's life's as cheap as beast's.'*

'Quote me no more of Will's words, Tooley!' Heminges says.

But I have more:

> *'But, for true need,*
> *You heavens, give me that patience, patience I need.*
> *You see me here, you gods, a poor old man,*
> *As full of grief as age, wretched in both.'*

'You can turn the words whichever way you like, it won't ever make them true,' Heminges says, eyes down, hands pressed into his papers.

'If you print the words, people will make more use of them than you can imagine,' I say.

'I could report you for sodomy, if you do not want to share what it is that you hold,' Heminges says, still unable to see me.

'I would rather die a happy sodomite than an unhappy player,' I say.

'You are very good with words, Master Tooley,' he says.

'Women like me must wield words the way men like you wield swords.'

Heminges shakes his head for a moment, and when he starts to speak, it is soft and clear.

'You think you're the only man here who needs? Look at us, Condell and me. His face is so thick with paint because he thinks it means the young clowns will have another year behind him. He has eight families to feed with his shares. I have more, and soon I will not be able to see the roles to con them into my receptacle, and they will find a way to get me out of this playhouse, unless you give me those words and you come with us in this printing plan.'

He has not noticed, but I am already standing back on the earthen floor before him.

'How bad are your eyes?' I ask.

'Sometimes I confuse the names of the little ones playing at my feet. They laugh at me, but soon I will be confusing everyone else, and I won't be able to hide it,' he says.

'I've already said you can have the words,' I say.

'And I've already said you can have your name on the book,' he replies.

IT is 2010 and when I arrive home from my new day job as the editor of a lifestyle magazine, there are several messages on the answering machine.

I hit the play button and make myself something to eat. The first is from the artistic director of a theatre company on the coast. She is sounding very upbeat and keen, says she'd like to show *Merely Players* to another theatre company in the city. She reckons they'll be interested, and asks me to call her ASAP.

The next is the artistic director of the city company. He sounds less animated, languid, almost, says he tried my mobile number but it rang out. I roll my eyes about the terrible mobile phone coverage in our area just as he indicates he is reading *Merely Players* today.

The next message sounds like a third artistic director, but it is, in fact, the second one again. The difference is he's now read the play, and he realises it's a script I sent to him over a year prior. He wants to make that point very, very clearly: the exact month and year he first saw 'the material', and it comes with a proprietorial tone, asking me to call him ASAP.

I ring on the landline and get straight through to him.

'We saw this play first,' he keeps saying, until I respond with a clear affirmation. He sounds keen but still smooth, a little clipped, like someone not used to being surprised by anything.

For more than two years, *Merely Players* has been rejected by every major and minor theatre company in the country.

The only interest the script has garnered to that point has been from artistic directors who have contacted me, sharing their relief that my play is not the same as the 'great idea we have for a play based on the work of Shakespeare', which is their excuse for why they cannot produce mine.

One of the country's pre-eminent companies ran an annual play development program for epic plays informed by the work of William Shakespeare. They rejected *Merely Players* in favour of a series of works that never made it to any stage.

Another state theatre company declined to offer development funds to a single script from more than three hundred ideas sent to them, including mine.

But never before or since have I felt the heat of competition over my intellectual property. I am so out of my depth I say yes to everything.

For once I forget about stuffing my face with food and take a turn in the garden with the dogs. As the light disappears, the evening fills with the kind of creative potential every writer dreams of.

MERELY PLAYERS

MASTER Condell does what clowns do. He places himself between me and Heminges and he speaks: 'You both need the other, that has been clear from the minute Master Tooley returned.'

'You don't even know my name,' I say. 'I had to leave the convent because they found out I was not a real woman, so I wrote to Mrs Burbage, to see if my Master would take me back, but it was not as Nicholas Tooley,' I say.

Condell makes it sound more than it is. 'There, I am right. Master Tooley... or whatever your name is, need not fear, the King's Men will not put him... her, out on the street. We'll put her to work in the playhouse.'

'I confess there is another reason,' I say. 'When I went to remember my lines, I did not have them so well as I used.'

'It has been ten years,' Condell says, smiling.

'Nay, it is more than time. If I wait too long, I fear my words will go like Burbage's,' I say.

'A brave confession for a player. And you, Heminges?' Condell says.

'What?' Heminges asks.

'What do you confess?'

'I, confess?' Heminges says, laughing. 'I confess that when the sun rose this day, I never saw it would set with things the way they are.'

'And... what else?' Condell asks, every part of his face wider than it was.

'What else? I confess I never thought there would come a day when a man in a skirt would hold so much in his hands as he does, right now, before us,' Heminges says.

'And... cough it up, Heminges,' Condell says, now droll.

'And that man would ask so little in return,' Heminges manages, wiping his mouth.

'Man?' Condell says, back to clowning. 'All I see here is you, and me, and one fine lady of the stage!'

'I cannot make believe Tooley is a real woman off the stage. What if one of the other men notices me calling him by a woman's name?' Heminges asks.

'You could just pretend it's your bad eyes,' Condell replies.

'I don't think I have it in me.'

'Oh, it won't take much, just two little words,' Condell says, beckoning me to come closer.

'Which two?' Heminges asks.

I take my cue, bending into a curtsy, putting my hand out for Heminges to kiss.

'Mistress Wilkinson, very pleased to make your acquaintance, Master Heminges,' I say.

Heminges does not move, so I make more of the moment.

'It's half right. Have you forgotten? Master Shakespeare called me that when he picked me for Juliet,' I say.

'Wilkinson?' Heminges asks.

'Aye. I was just thirteen, and he did not want my mama to pluck me off the stage if the Puritans found out Juliet was a boy by the name of Tooley. The Burbage women have always been happy to call me Mistress Wilkinson, in public.'

'And Mrs Burbage knows nothing, about you and her husband?'

'Oh, I think she has always suspected, but she has said nothing,' I say. 'She only wants someone to stay close to Dickie, to get him home. That is enough for me. If there's something to play, I can do it. It will suit me

MERELY PLAYERS

better than trying to fool the priests.'

'There's a man,' Condell says.

Heminges looks between us, then goes as if to shake my outstretched hand. 'There's a King's Man,' he says.

At the last moment, I turn my hand back over.

'Here's nothing but a player,' I say.

And Master Heminges kisses it.

Sans everything

IT IS 2011 and I am sitting downstage at the small studio theatre used by the city theatre company. The actors who've just completed a rehearsed reading of *Merely Players* have given the play its best chance before an interested crowd of friends and industry folk.

All day, we've worked the script with a young director who knows his stuff. My lengthy, heaving early drafts have been dramatically cut into shape. What began as an epic has been altered through dramaturgy into something more match-fit to compete in the Sydney theatre industry.

In my heart I am happy. Spending a day in the company of actors very experienced in Shakespeare has proven the premise of my idea: older actors remember the lines they have played on the stage, long, long after the show is over.

The actors playing Burbage and Tooley have shown me how wonderful that great, hidden relationship will be when it makes the stage. Both men portrayed the public hunger for fame and validation in these characters, and their private desires. They used every old theatre trick in the book to work the scenes as far as they will go script-in-hand, and they served the writing so well that it's incredibly touching to benefit from their expertise.

The actors playing Heminges and Condell inhabited that enduring friendship with all its competitive moments, and the right level of urgency and desperation.

By the time the show was over, my head bursting with ideas, I got nervous. As soon as they'd arrived ahead of the rehearsed reading, I'd clocked the row of seasoned professionals in the front row, and spent much of the evening pushing away my fears that one or more of them was an expert on Shakespeare who would be able to unravel my plot with one hitherto unknown fact or some academic discovery I'd missed in my eight years of work on *Merely Players*.

But, facing them from the actor's perspective, from the stage, I am able to look them in the eye. They have no questions on authenticity, only helpful musings on wanting more of me and less of Shakespeare.

The artistic director sits at the side, on the steps, not on a chair, giving him an air of departure that I should have taken note of at the time.

When everyone has had their say, he poses a question, feeding the answer to me like an offstage prompt.

'Is this play a comedy, or a tragedy?' he asks, opening his gaze to the assembled minds. 'If it's a comedy, you'll have a hit on your hands,' he feels the need to add.

It's my only moment of reticence, because I am experienced enough to know he wants only one answer. He's made it that obvious.

Perhaps all playwrights are subjected to a similar public intervention? I have no idea about the ramifications of my answer, just that the black and white world of the 21st-century playhouse is revealing itself to me in a rush, where comedies, with casts of four at the most, have the most potential to make it as far as a mainstage production.

My literary journey has been brought down to a case of basic mathematics.

MY hand is still in Heminges'. It seems that now he has me, he does not want to let me go.

Condell speaks first. 'We will ink every man's name

after Shakespeare and Burbage, in the order that he came into his shares, whether he lives or has gone to his grave.'

'That's fair,' I say, trying to draw my hand back. 'You can ink Nicholas Tooley as though he were dead.'

'Just one page, so it won't add much to the cost,' Condell says, trying to get a reaction out of Heminges.

'Agreed,' Heminges finally says, letting my hand fall. 'Now, help me with the pages, there is no time to do more than bundle them together.'

Condell nods and bends to the work, but my senses have been filled with alarm for some time.

'I'll help you search after I've done what I've been needing to do since I came off,' I say, and draw into the privy, pulling the curtain shut behind me.

In the darkness, I gather up my skirts in order to piss. When it flows, I exhale, and I listen. The sound of paper fills the small space, and I can hear every word the other men are saying.

'We'll have to play the poet, you and I,' Heminges says.

'How so?' Condell asks.

'We'll have to fill in the gaps, and there'll be plenty. Not just with dross, with poetry as good as Will Shakespeare's.'

'Well, as long as you don't play the pedant too often,' Condell warns.

'What do you mean?' Heminges asks.

By the sound of his voice, I imagine Condell is mocking Heminges when he says: '"Write down the page, put every character's name in a large hand, so it can be seen. Are you putting in the gestures and moves?".'

'I never said that,' Heminges says, mortified.

'Did,' Condell replies.

'I would never say "moves", I'd say "enter" and "exit".'

'That's better,' Condell says.

'Now you're sounding just like a printer,' Heminges adds.

I finish off and realise I have piss on my fingers, so I reach down in the dark to where a pile of papers sits, and pull one off to clean myself. Just as I allow the light back by drawing the curtain, I see the handwriting on the piece I have just used.

'Here's more play,' I say, bending.

'What, just sitting in the privy?' Condell asks.

'Aye, the privy paper... there is plenty,' I say, pulling the curtain across enough to find every page on the floor. In the light, I see more pages, lining the inside of the pot, and take it by the handle, trying to avoid its rank smell.

'There's more, in there?' Heminges asks, his face filling with dread.

Holding my fingers over my nose, I nod.

IT is 2012 and I am escaping the city on the train, again. It is winter, so the night has closed in early and the shadows of Sydney's western suburbs are absorbing the last of the light that disappeared long ago below the dark block of the Blue Mountains.

I want to disappear into that darkness and never have to emerge.

Three days have been allocated to this second round of rehearsed readings of *Merely Players*, the last for another public reading.

The whole first day has been a process of stripping my idea to the core. At one end of the table, the young director, who was in my year at NIDA (and also didn't remember my heavily-fringed geek), sits with younger actors who are incredibly proactive with ideas.

Barely twenty minutes into the read, one of them was on his feet rewriting the opening scene and acting it out for us, suggesting it would make a great film. We laughed, but all he achieved was avoiding reading my version of the opening scene, which is why we were all being paid to be there.

Up my end of the table, a row of very familiar older faces performed their roles impeccably, inhabiting the characters with clues they discovered on the page, with an added attitude here or a flourish there, lifting the work higher, showing its potential; and they did it consistently again and again, no matter how many times they were asked.

Walking back from lunch through a nearby arcade, I saw through the glass wall of the empty office we're spending these three days in. Outside the corporate kitchen, the younger actors were laughing and making drinks or seeing to their salads.

I had done my research about the cast. Like many struggling Sydney actors, a couple on this gig had branched into writing and producing to diversify income streams. It would be a big ask for them to separate acting from writing, and that is what they must do today, yet I sensed they would not.

One of them, the 'opening scene' guy, proceeds to spend the whole time rewriting, constantly avoiding characterising his role for my benefit.

The artistic director misses most of that, because he doesn't stay for the afternoon session. The director isn't assertive enough to direct his actor to inhabit my lines, not rewrite them, and by day's end we have descended into writing by committee, during which I am asked: 'Are you okay?' once every thirty minutes.

I guess they don't really want to hear the truth. We're all getting paid, no matter what shape the play is in by the end.

On the train, I wonder if I should just stay up all night and rewrite the whole thing. It would probably be possible. In the end I rewrite just the opening, knowing how tiny changes will have so many ramifications for the rest of the storyline that I'd need weeks to get the script ready for a reading.

The next morning, the cast is happier with their new opening. They rip through it and have a laugh before their coffee break, and I'm left wondering exactly when Australian writers began to be considered the worst enemies of our own work, and why this terrible dance with play development began.

'You're taking this all very well,' the oldest actor, playing Burbage, tells me over coffee. He has given me so many ideas in his characterisation I joke with him that I'll have to give him a writing credit.

It's not a comedy or a tragedy, it's just a bloody mess, but I know I will rewrite it, as I always do. I can make it whatever shape the artistic director wants, whatever length, style, cast number and scope, if only he will come clean about what it is he does want.

In one of my breaks I call my friends and ask them to forget about coming to the planned reading. I sense my work is about to be damaged, perhaps irreversibly.

When we wrap this difficult, unnecessary process, I promise to have a full rewrite done in a fortnight, and I work like a dog to get it done.

But instead of ending the year with *Merely Players* being picked up for the promised mainstage production,

ACTING LIKE SHAKESPEARE REALLY MATTERS

I find out it's been completely dropped when I receive next year's season brochure and do not see my play listed anywhere. Cowards.

HEMINGES and Condell look at me over the top of the piss pot.

'You'll have to read it, I can't see a thing, remember?' Heminges says.

Condell rolls his eyes and says to me: 'We'll both do it. Hold it steady,' and he reads the damp top page:

'Is love a tender thing? It is too rough,
Too rude, too boisterous, and it pricks like thorn...'

Master Heminges takes the thread, and speaks:

'If love be rough with you, be rough with love;
Prick love for pricking, and you beat love down.'

His eyes are ablaze: 'That's Mercutio.'

'*Romeo and Juliet*,' Condell says.

'How much of it?' Heminges asks.

I hold up the pile of privy paper.

'Looks like most of it, apart from what's been used already on every man's pissy fingers, and we could piece those together.'

IT is 2014 and I sit in the shade of spreading trees at the beach, a band of really hot sand runs between me and the gentle waves that cool this lagoon-like tidal shore of Coochiemudlo. The dogs are sniffing through the low hanging branches, following the signs of soldier crabs.

I have replaced the well-travelled train journey between Sydney and the Blue Mountains with a ferry ride across Queensland's Moreton Bay, whenever day jobs demand it.

MERELY PLAYERS

Richard and I have made what Australians have lately called a sea-change, which is not a buzz word created by any real estate institute – it comes straight from Shakespeare's *The Tempest*.

'Full fathom five thy father lies,
Of his bones are coral made,
Those are pearls that were his eyes,
Nothing of him that doth fade,
But doth suffer a sea-change,
into something rich and strange,
Sea-nymphs hourly ring his knell,
Ding-dong.
Hark! now I hear them, ding-dong, bell.'

Leaving the Blue Mountains after my three-decade association with the region saw me shuffle off almost everything I owned.

We started again, which is exactly what I did when I threw aside the entire contents of the soundly rejected and over-developed versions of *Merely Players* and went back to my original inspiration.

I'd consulted the Australian Writers Guild and found I had the right to ask both artistic directors who'd shown an interest if they'd like to option my play. The coastal company considered the terms of my email and professionally declined. The city company bitterly dodged my offer, and, after the two-month time period expired with nothing but silence, I claimed back all ownership of my idea.

I looked back into my Baroque mental picture, sketched during a speedy lesson in Elizabethan theatre, and I realised how in all the years since it was formed, I had walked right through the fourth wall.

Two dimensions had become three, as I reinvented myself from a geeky kid skilled at visual arts, into a player who'd stood on stages and performed the words of Shakespeare.

But I'd also leaped into the void, facing the crowd as honestly as I could about my true nature.

Encouraged onward by the stark, sapphire blue of the bay, where all things are laid bare under the elements, I made a study of storytelling. Walking alone on the beaches, I ruminated on some of the world's great plots, with a view to improving my own.

It took me another two years to completely rewrite, but the penultimate version of *Merely Players* is very simple. I worked without all the show-business chatter, my primary aim being to entertain myself, and today I've walked to the corner of the island the hour that I knew it was complete, thoughts of Viola in *Twelfth Night*, washed-up on another island – Illyria.

'What country, friends, is this?'

It's a place where my characters – my brainchildren – sit in my heart, as real as friends, so ready I could burst with pride at their achievements, their primary one being endurance. Only this week have I become sure they are complete, when I notice I've stopped worrying about them as I drift off to sleep in the divine heat.

I've earned the right to call myself a writer. For the first time in my life I have an office. Novels, non-fiction, journalism, all come pouring out. I have so much to say, and, as it turns out, I do not leave the publication of it all to chance like Shakespeare did. With editing, design and promotional skills picked up over my entire career, I do it all myself.

What failures need I fear now, in the uncharted territory of the wordsmith?

Returning home through the shade of the wetlands, the dogs at my heels, I chuckle at how even William

MERELY PLAYERS

Shakespeare, if he were alive and writing, with his casts of thousands and his unsurpassed ability to blend comedy and tragedy, would never get a new play produced on an Australian stage these days.

Without Heminges and Condell to champion his work, compile it, restore it, find sponsorship and forge a relationship with London's best-equipped printer (who had previously tried to rip them off); despite questionable remnant originals owned by several savvy stationers, Shakespeare would have avoided the label of literary genius altogether.

We know little enough about the man whose work is performed as commonly for its quality as it is for the fact that nobody owns it and it costs nothing for a license to play it on any stage in the world.

We know even less about Heminges and Condell. Apart from historians, who ruminate more on Shakespeare's work than what saved it, I know very few people – just a few actors, who also write a little – who are aware of what these players pulled off.

No-one else really gives a shit about one of literature's most inconspicuous achievements.

From this island, I will go on to face more years of rejection for *Merely Players*, from LGBTI theatre development programs in two countries to international play competitions and theatre companies across three continents.

I will get a very strong bite from a literary agent in London, who will renege, via Twitter, on his agreement to meet me, just as Richard and I are in Paris about to get on the Eurostar.

When I press this agent about why, he will claim plays set in the past are impossible to sell, in a West End season bursting with period pieces.

ACTING LIKE SHAKESPEARE REALLY MATTERS

One of these will be the production of Shakespeare's Roman-era *Titus Andronicus* that we'll delight in at Shakespeare's Globe during a spring afternoon by the Thames.

Intermittent showers will fall through the Globe's open-air span and dampen our enraptured faces, sitting in the first row, looking over the heads of the crowd in the playhouse yard.

I will let most of the crowd leave before taking in the great wooden frame of the emptying building, and I'll make a wish that all the inspiration, dreaming, work, research, loss and hope will one day be worth it.

But there will be no scene for me, like Julie Powell's in *Julie and Julia*, where the struggling writer returns home to phone messages from publishers and agents falling over themselves to take their career to the next level.

I'll become nothing more than an afterthought I'll put into my own play to make it work.

The powerlessness that breathed life into *Merely Players* will never really leave me; although, by definition, if a protagonist is better off at the end than they were at the beginning, the story can never be seen as a tragedy.

So I'll breathe more life into Nicholas Tooley, I'll pour every moment of my disenfranchisement into Mistress Wilkinson's story and fit the politics around the shape that Shakespeare left us, with all his cross-dressing heroines who could only have been played by men, and trans women.

I'll give Tooley the greatest power in the story, something as invisible and seemingly worthless as memory, and allow it to be wielded out of love.

If anyone ever has the courage to stage *Merely Players* as it's written, they'll discover it's all there on the page.

MERELY PLAYERS

I HOLD in my hand what looks like most of Will Shakespeare's *Romeo and Juliet*. Not a printer's copy of it, but Will Shakespeare's very own. The rest is in the piss pot.

Heminges is trying his best to collect all the play pages together. The ones with Master Burbage's stage blood all over them, and those which were wrapped around today's pies from the playhouse bakery, scattered with various papers from Burbage's table. I can see more paper than earth on the floor around us.

'If you leave now, you can still beat the printer's boys to the Stationer!' Condell says.

'I'm supposed to be on, in the last scene,' Heminges says, shoving papers in the box.

'What say I add a new jig to the end of *Romeo and Juliet*, fifteen verses, with plenty of new words in a complicated double-rhyme, which the printer's boys won't want to miss a single word of,' Condell says. 'Will that give you a head start?'

'I could be on the other side of the river by the time you bring it down,' Heminges says, managing to get another armful of Shakespeare into the box.

I make for the third step and cast an eye across the stage. Right down the front, the last of the day's light making a halo out of his thinning hair, my Master is holding the crowd in his hand.

'There is no need. Master Burbage is on,' I say.

'What's he doing?' Heminges asks, sitting on the lid of the box to make more room for the two wedges of paper in either hand.

'He's padding it out,' I say.

'What's he playing?' Heminges asks.

I can tell by my Master's gestures what he is up to.

'Bits of *Hamlet*. The printer's boys are looking at one

another,' I say.

Condell smiles, another pile of papers in his hand ready for stuffing. 'He knows what he's doing, the old devil.'

'Now he's starting on bits of *Macbeth*,' I say.

'How did he know we needed time?' Heminges asks, helping Condell stuff the last piles into the sides of the box.

'An addled man still has ears and eyes. You might ask him for help in the morning, and he'll deliver it, but not till the afternoon,' I say, as Heminges takes the pages I forgot I was still holding in my hands.

'There is enough of *Romeo and Juliet* here for you to say it is complete,' I tell him.

Heminges points to the piss pot. 'What about the bits in here?'

'Well... that's the rest of it,' I say, shrugging.

Condell laughs. 'The stationers cannot complain what form the words are in, now can they?'

'Nay, it's never word-perfect,' I say.

'Take *Romeo and Juliet*, go!' Condell tells Heminges. 'We'll follow with the rest.'

'We're taking all the plays to the Stationers' Guild, tonight?' Heminges asks.

'Why not?' Condell says.

'All these bloodied and pissy papers, matched with our failing memories... now that we have agreed to it I scarcely see how it can be done. It will take us years to make a book of all Will Shakespeare's plays,' Heminges says.

'Years of making trouble, and it's bound to get us back upstairs, you said so yourself,' Condell says. 'Come, Tooley, we'll need to use Burbage's box to carry it all. When the printers are done with all this it will certainly be ready for Mrs Burbage's fire.'

'I'll get out of my women's weeds first,' I say.

'Nay, come as you are, it matters not,' Heminges says from the stairs.

'Are you still here?' Condell says. 'Go!'

Heminges looks between me and Condell, smiles, and disappears into the light, bearing papers under one arm and the piss pot in the other.

'I don't know about you, but I say Shakespeare's *Romeo and Juliet* stinks!' Condell says, wrangling the handle at one end of the box.

'Aye, you could say every one of us left our mark on it,' I say, taking the other handle.

We lift it up the first two steps, and though it is heavy, we both know without saying it that we'll manage, this late afternoon, to get the plays of William Shakespeare to the Stationers' Guild on the other side of the Thames.

Condell is on the third step, and judging by his face I know what he is looking at on the stage.

'Look at Burbage,' Condell says. 'You could almost believe he played us all, getting you back, letting us argue about shares, and waiting, until Master Heminges' printing plan was back on the table.'

I know straight away what I want to say:

'All the world's a stage, and all the men and women...'

Condell joins me in the final two words:

'...merely players.'

'That's my line... well, it was my line,' he says, smiling.

'We should go,' I say. 'I'll help you to the river. I want to be here when he comes off.'

Condell lifts the box ahead of me, and, as I pass the gap in the ceiling which reveals the stage, I see Burbage. Darkness is already gathering at the edges of the playhouse, but there is light coming from every monkey's

ACTING LIKE SHAKESPEARE REALLY MATTERS

face, as Burbage speaks:

> *'Tomorrow, and tomorrow, and tomorrow,*
> *Creeps in this petty pace from day to day*
> *To the last syllable of recorded time,*
> *And all our yesterdays have lighted fools*
> *The way to dusty death...'*

When we reach the top, I hear that he has forgotten his lines, so he draws in a great breath, right from the roof, and he goes on:

> *'Out, out, brief candle!*
> *Life's but a walking shadow, a poor player*
> *That struts and frets his hour upon the stage*
> *And then is heard no more. It is a tale*
> *Told by an idiot, full of sound and fury,*
> *Signifying nothing.'*

'Dear lad, believe it;
For they shall yet belie thy happy years
That say thou art a man. Diana's lip
Is not more smooth and rubious, thy small pipe
Is as the maiden's organ, shrill and sound,
And all is semblative a woman's part.'

William Shakespeare, *Twelfth Night*, Act 1, Scene IV

LGBTI Labour's Lost

A case for transgender players

OUTING LESBIAN, GAY, bisexual, transgender and intersex (LGBTI) performers has long been an emotive and legal tightrope for historians, but 400 years since William Shakespeare's death, it's time to look where academics have feared to glance.

When Shakespeare's fellow actors John Heminges and Henry Condell oversaw the publication of his complete works in 1623, they included a page of "The names of the Principall Actors in all these Playes".

It was never illegal for women to perform on the stage in Shakespeare's era, but it was seen as an unthinkable moral breach akin to prostitution. The solution was to cast boys in the female roles.

So of this list of twenty-six male performers, which must include those who played heroines from Juliet to Cleopatra, which fellows donned the skirts?

Ruling out those credited with male roles leaves a cluster of men who began their careers as 'boy players' and wouldn't register on any acting roll of honour – Alexander Cooke, John Shancke, Samuel Crosse, Nathan Field and Nicholas Tooley – yet all were shareholders in England's premier theatre company The King's Men.

Henry VIII's *Buggery Act* of 1533 ensured LGBTIs remained invisible for centuries in the performing arts, however, it's simply not credible to assume all the men on Shakespeare's cast list were straight.

So I'll add historical evidence to conjecture and show how easy it is to make room for a same sex-attracted transgender woman within a Shakespearean playhouse, and why she left almost no trace.

The record shows that twice-widowed Susan Tooley was on the market for husband number three in 1592. If we imagine her 10-year-old son, Nicholas, showed early signs of acting skill, we can paint Susan as a stage mother who made use of a known link the boy's father's family had to the Stratford-upon-Avon Shakespeares.

If the Tooleys – landed Warwickshire gentry – agreed to make the introductions that got the child off Susan's genteel apron strings and into the hotbed of sodomy and vice that the Elizabethan playhouse was considered to be, I imagine they enforced one important condition. The boy, by that time listed in the records of London's Court of Orphans as 'orphan Tooley', would have needed an assumed name.

We know from his will that Nicholas Tooley had an alias – the undistinguished surname 'Wilkinson'. Perhaps it was coined for him in 1595, when a gifted lad was required for a crucial role in a new play?

Pamphlets from that decade reveal the playhouses came under the most intense Puritanical fire against boys cross-dressing on the public stage. If it was 'orphan Tooley' who appeared opposite Richard Burbage in the world premiere of *Romeo and Juliet*, the 13-year-old may wisely have cross-dressed as 'Nick Wilkinson'.

Imagining the production was a hit allows us to cast 'player Wilkinson' opposite Burbage in Shakespeare's regular new plays. The workload, and the pressure to maintain a slight physique, may have led the teenager, twice in 1599, to seek treatment from Simon Forman, London's leading astrologer and herbalist. Forman's notes reveal Tooley complained to him of "melancholy... moch gnawing in his stomak & stuffing in his Lungs."

We know Shakespeare attempted to dampen the Puritan inferno by writing a batch of heroines who cross-dressed as men; but this could also have been a way to make performing lead female roles easier on one talented, ailing adolescent. The playwright let audiences in on the laughs, however, and created some of the best homoerotic scenes in theatre history, in *Twelfth Night* and *As You Like It*.

When 'orphan Tooley' reached his majority in 1603, Richard Burbage applied to the Court of Orphans to have him indentured. Clearly, 'player Wilkinson' had become indispensable, and since the authority had no choice but to use his birth name on the paperwork, Nicholas Tooley finally emerged as a player.

Under the terms of his apprenticeship, the young man was accommodated by the wider Burbage family, London's leading theatrical dynasty.

Surely it was the relentless playhouse work, wrangling not only his own scripts but also his master's, performing before enormous crowds in the pre-eminent popular entertainments of the day, that led to Tooley's elevation to shareholder of The King's Men by 1605.

For anyone on the payroll to make a career as a leading lady would have drawn plenty of negative attention; but Shakespeare's next move suggests he recognised the dramatic potential of one man's ability to convincingly inhabit feminine authority, passion and lust.

When the playwright dropped the cross-dressing of comic female heroines and created his most complex female roles – Desdemona (1603), Lady Macbeth and Cleopatra (both 1606) – one review showed the impact.

In a performance of *Othello* by the King's Men in

1610, a consummate actress fooled diarist Henry Jackson into writing: "She always acted the matter very well, in her death moved us still more greatly; when lying in bed she implored the pity of those watching with her countenance alone."

Was this Desdemona played by Nicholas Tooley at the height of 'her' powers?

Onstage gender boundaries were being tested. In 1611, Londoners were thrilled and scandalised by the performance of a woman at the Fortune Theatre – Mary Frith, alias Moll Cutpurse, the infamous 'Roaring Girl'.

Her subsequent confession to the Consistory Court states: "She told the company there p[re]sent that she thought many of them were of the opinion that she was a man, but if any of them would come to her lodging they should finde that she is a woman & some other immodest & lascivious speaches she also vsed at that time And also sat there vppon the stage in the publique viewe of all the people there p[rese]nte in mans apparell & playd vppon her lute & sange a songe."

Mary's arrest, public shaming and penance were the playhouse gossip of the 1612 season and surely struck fear in the heart of every cross-dressing performer.

Now 30, Tooley was overlooked for the title role in a play by the newest writer on the scene, John Webster, whose *The Duchess of Malfi* ushered in the next generation of boy players, playwrights and shareholders.

My story, *Merely Players*, drew inspiration from this pivotal moment in Western theatre history.

Tooley's one documented attempt at playing a male role was in Webster's hit tragedy, while witnessing his replacement emerge; so it's not a stretch to imagine his melancholy returned with force as he struggled to maintain his identity in the playhouse.

LGBTI LABOUR'S LOST

It's also common for an intense period of playing passionate lovers to lay fertile ground for a relationship offstage; so it's not incredible to suggest that Tooley and Burbage had an ongoing affair that came under threat as master's career continued while apprentice's declined.

My story has Tooley making a gender transition while disappearing for years into one of the few places that I believe would have taken him in – London's Convent of Saint Helen. Here, she may have fooled the nuns into thinking she was a woman. The name I imagine was easiest for her to adopt was one she'd already used – Mistress Wilkinson.

After hearing that her old master is not well, I have her strolling back into the Globe playhouse in 1619, where she uncovers much hanging in the balance.

Before his death in 1623, the never-married Nicholas Tooley used his birth name to legitimise significant financial gifts to a coterie of women, including his master's sister-in-law Elizabeth Burbage, "in whose howse I doe now lodge as a remembrance of my love in respect of her motherlie care over mee". He stipulated the funds were to be paid into the womens' "owne proper hands" and not to any husband.

The document reveals a man who spent much time in the company of a large number of women, and knew the legal impediment that marriage placed on daughters, wives and sisters inheriting monies independently.

But Tooley also signed a codicil identifying himself as "Nicholas Wilkinson alias Nicholas Tooley", which no historian has ever thought to investigate as a cisgender dead name.

Any number of participants in Western theatre's groundbreaking era could have been LGBTIs, it's simply a matter of ending the academic silence.

MERELY PLAYERS

Aliases, gender dysphoria, cross-dressing, bisexuality, homosexuality and performing have always gone hand in hand, and apart from sharing the stage when cisgender English women finally got public support for bursting onto the stage in the 1660s, in 400 years not much has changed behind the scenes.

Merely Players

A two-act play

Characters

Mistress Wilkinson, alias Nicholas Tooley
Richard Burbage
John Heminges
Henry Condell

*The action takes place backstage at London's Globe Theatre
over one afternoon in early 1619*

Act One

Beneath the stage of London's Globe Theatre, 1619. A cramped mess of packing cases, baskets, costume rails and props. Above, the floorboards of the stage allow uneven slits of light, and dust, to fall through, and we sense the sounds and shadows of the end of a performance.

A woman enters down primitive steps, carrying a basket. She peers through a gap in the ceiling near the stairs, through which light and shadows fall from the Globe stage. She's amused by what she sees, dusts-off a stool, sits in a shaft of light and takes out a small piece of mirror. Her face dissatisfies her. She wipes off her make-up, and starts again...

TOOLEY: "God gave you a face, but you make yourself a better one" (*pause*)... is that right? "God gave you your face, and yet you make yourself another". (*Pause, then, addressing herself in the mirror*) Mistress Wilkinson, you have forgotten your lines! "God gave you one face, and you make yourself another," that's right. That's word-perfect.

There is a huge round of applause upstairs, and she curtsies to her own imaginary crowd.

A commotion on the stairs as RICHARD BURBAGE, JOHN HEMINGES and HENRY CONDELL enter in comic costumes, CONDELL with the white face of a classic Elizabethan clown. All are in their fifties, have mobility issues, and are full of after-show swagger.

BURBAGE dumps his hat and props into the woman's arms, grapples with his breeches and goes straight for a makeshift privy behind a curtain. HEMINGES and CONDELL wait their turn, in some agitation, starting to remove their costumes and also dumping them on (cont'd) (cont'd) the woman, who starts hanging them up.

BURBAGE: *(pissing)* Sweet relief... get the barrel open, lads.

CONDELL: *(unloading a small barrel)* Aye, but hurry it up in there Burbage.

BURBAGE: Just wait your turn Condell, I might get another call.

HEMINGES: There's no calls yet.

BURBAGE: Oh, they'll call for me Heminges, just wait for it.

Another large round of applause from the Globe stage. The players go tense with listening for calls. BURBAGE finishes pissing, emerges, looking for something.

BURBAGE: *(cont'd)* If you two buggers are going to keep pissing in my pot, be sure to replace the privy paper when you've used it all!

BURBAGE fetches a wad of papers from his things and hands them to HEMINGES as he rushes into the privy.

HEMINGES: *(with great relief)* Good of you, Burbage, to allow us a share of the room.

BURBAGE: My private dressing room.

CONDELL: Private doss-house, more like.

BURBAGE: Can it, clown.

CONDELL opens the barrel's spigot. Then a call goes up. Cries of "Bur-bage, Bur-bage, Bur-bage!" fills the space.

BURBAGE: *(cont'd)* They're calling for me, but I cannot go after playing so small a part.

CONDELL: It might have been a small part, but the crowd loved you, you must go!

BURBAGE: Only if you think I should...

HEMINGES finishes and wipes himself on paper.

HEMINGES: We'll follow you, go on!

CONDELL: Wait for me, I'm about to burst!

HEMINGES: Burbage cannot wait, they're calling him!

ACT ONE

CONDELL: I'll leave it then, we'll go... go!

BURBAGE leads HEMINGES and CONDELL up the steps to the Globe stage. The woman completes hanging costumes, then seeks out the privy. Furtively, she goes to squat over it, gathering her skirts to do so. She sighs, looks nervously to the stairs, then pisses in the privy standing up.

It becomes clearer that this is NICHOLAS TOOLEY, a former boy player now pushing forty. Her carriage, voice, physique: everything about her is transgender female.

A commotion and HEMINGES, CONDELL and BURBAGE return, exhausted. CONDELL dives straight for the privy in desperation.

BURBAGE: No more. I can do no more. Pour me a drink.

TOOLEY pours everyone a drink and hands them around.

CONDELL: I need to be empty before I take any more on board!

BURBAGE: Quiet! (*Another call of "Bur-bage, Bur-bage, Bur-bage!"*) I couldn't possibly manage another climb.

HEMINGES: Of course you could.

BURBAGE: What about the men who played the leads, what would they think of me, hogging all the calls?

HEMINGES: They're not calling for the other men, they're calling for the great Richard Burbage. That's why they come to the Globe playhouse, to see Richard Burbage, the shining light of The King's Men, England's finest company of players. Get up there!

Pause, the chant is louder. CONDELL finishes in the privy, wiping off on paper.

BURBAGE: Pour me a drink.

TOOLEY does so. BURBAGE downs it in one, then prepares to climb the steps.

BURBAGE: (*cont'd*) When I get up top, leave me, I (*cont'd*)

MERELY PLAYERS

BURBAGE: (*cont'd*) can manage from there.
> *They all climb. TOOLEY starts preparing a round of drinks from the barrel. As CONDELL and HEMINGES return, the crowd applauds BURBAGE.*

CONDELL: Shouldn't we wait up top and help him down?

HEMINGES: He's better at getting down by himself.

CONDELL: Nay, when the crowd's calling, it takes twenty years off him.

HEMINGES: Watch for him, and help if he needs it.

CONDELL: Aye, but I need a drink.
> *TOOLEY hands them both one.*

BURBAGE: (*from upstairs*) Heminges, Condell, come, assist!
> *HEMINGES and CONDELL shrug and down their drinks, then help BURBAGE.*

BURBAGE: (*cont'd*) It's only that I hurt my knees, doing all that kneeling in the play.

HEMINGES: You need to sit down before the next play. Woman, a drink for Master Burbage.
> *TOOLEY brings them all fresh drinks as HEMINGES and CONDELL sit BURBAGE in his large chair.*

BURBAGE: Cheers.

HEMINGES: Cheers.

CONDELL: To our next play.

BURBAGE: What are we doing?

TOOLEY: You're playing *Romeo and Juliet*.
> *The players are taken aback.*

HEMINGES: The washer woman knows what play we're doing, but we players do not?

CONDELL: Heminges, hold off, we haven't had a whore call on us in ages!

HEMINGES: Come to think of it, we haven't had a washer woman see to us in ages.

ACT ONE

BURBAGE: Never speak of the washer women as whores!

TOOLEY: Master Condell, there isn't gold enough in your pocket for the likes of me.

CONDELL: I've gold enough, for a pretty lass. Come into the light. Let me see if you're worth it.

TOOLEY: *(acting)* "What's here? A cup, closed in my true love's hand? Poison, I see, hath been his timeless end. Oh churl! drunk all, and left no friendly drop to help me after? I will kiss thy lips." *(She kisses CONDELL)*

BURBAGE: She reminds me of my own Juliet.

CONDELL: *(trying to embrace TOOLEY)* A pretty scene, wench, but no woman plays on the stage. They would close us down for harbouring harlots!

TOOLEY: *(escaping)* I'm no washer woman, or a harlot, masters. We have all met before.

BURBAGE: I know the voice, but the face... can it be? Is it Master Tooley?

CONDELL: Master Tooley? *(Wiping off the kiss)* I would never have known you.

TOOLEY: I haven't gone by that name for a very long time.

HEMINGES: We haven't seen you at the playhouse these... ten years.

TOOLEY: Oh, they stopped writing parts for old women long ago.

HEMINGES: Ah, we must be playing *Antony and Cleopatra*, but your costume's not too queenly.

TOOLEY: Nay, I only came to visit Master Burbage, and it's *Romeo and Juliet*, I'm sure of it.

BURBAGE: What do you think of our new digs? Rougher than upstairs, but less crowded.

TOOLEY: Aye, it is a little different to the old days.

HEMINGES: Come, Tooley, they won't have got *(cont'd)*

HEMINGES: *(cont'd)* you back for Juliet. Cleopatra's more your thing.

TOOLEY: Nobody 'got me back', Master Heminges, and I read the playbill when I came in – it announces *Romeo and Juliet* as the afternoon play, clear as day.

HEMINGES: If it's Juliet, you'll be needing a veil or two.

HEMINGES and CONDELL stifle laughter.

TOOLEY: Master Burbage, do you know what is being played this afternoon?

BURBAGE: They never bring us a playbill down here. Someone will have to fetch it.

HEMINGES and CONDELL don't acknowledge that either of them could go.

TOOLEY: Since it seems I have lost my memory, I'd better go.

TOOLEY exits.

BURBAGE: You might have poured him a jar.

HEMINGES: Master Tooley never liked to carouse with the men, as I recall.

BURBAGE: Leave off the arguing, give him a chance to see if he likes it again.

HEMINGES: I thought he went to his grave, long ago. What's he doing back here?

BURBAGE: He is one of our very finest players.

HEMINGES: Did you ask him back?

BURBAGE: We've got to have our best players, if we're to fill a season.

HEMINGES: We'd all better be word-perfect, or Master Tooley – the playhouse pedant – will be on every man's back about getting his words right.

BURBAGE: Master Tooley is a long-standing member of this company, make him welcome.

HEMINGES: How long since he played on the stage?

ACT ONE

BURBAGE: Any one of our players can come and go as he pleases.

HEMINGES: Will he be attired in women's weeds as he comes and goes?

BURBAGE: Why? Are you thinking of lifting his skirt?

HEMINGES: We're none of us sodomites down here!

BURBAGE: Nay. Now, Heminges, you must pick up the pace at the end. You left me waiting again.

HEMINGES: I will. (*Aside to CONDELL*) And try not to damage my hearing...

BURBAGE: What was that?

HEMINGES: Nothing, I was just reminding Condell not to tread on all my lines.

BURBAGE: That's right. Condell, one laugh is good, two is great, but three is...

CONDELL: Greedy, I know. I can't help it. Once I get them giggling up the back, it comes washing over me like a wave and sets me off again.

BURBAGE: Like a cheap clown, you went after every other man's laughs. Do we have the play yet? Tooley, go and ask what we're playing.

CONDELL: You already sent him.

BURBAGE: I did?

CONDELL: Take it slow on the slop, old man.

BURBAGE: I could drink you under the table, both of you. (*TOOLEY enters with a roll of paper*) Ah, Tooley. What have we got?

TOOLEY: (*reading*) "The tragedy of *Romeo and Juliet*, featuring the great Richard Burbage and other players of The King's Men, at the Globe Playhouse in the afternoon, with entertainments before and after."

HEMINGES: I see you have not lost your perfect memory, Master Tooley.

TOOLEY: And you still have a liking for ordering every man about, Master Heminges.

BURBAGE: I shall have to say no to playing Romeo today. A message must be sent to young Joseph Taylor to come to the playhouse in an urgent fashion to go on for me, he's been drilled in the part.

HEMINGES: Master Taylor is already in the playhouse, Burbage.

BURBAGE: I thought they'd hired him out. (*To TOOLEY*) Did you see him?

TOOLEY: Aye.

BURBAGE: How's he looking, leggy?

TOOLEY: I didn't see his legs.

HEMINGES: They'll have young Nathan Field in for Juliet, since Master Tooley's not up to it.

BURBAGE: Nonsense. Tooley and I could play the lovers, even now (*HEMINGES and CONDELL stifle laughter*). In our day they could call any play, any play by William Shakespeare, at least, and we'd be ready after just donning our robes. Romeo, Othello, Lear... and Tooley as Juliet, Desdemona and Cordelia... any one of them. Young, leggy players don't have the goods these days.

CONDELL: I'm only too happy to get to the alehouse early after whatever little bit they give me.

BURBAGE: (*to HEMINGES and CONDELL*) Get yourselves up there and see what you're playing today. Tell them Master Tooley is available for Juliet.

TOOLEY: You need not tell them that.

BURBAGE: Nonsense, it's your role. If they want to put another man on in your place, they must ask you first. Tell Master Taylor he had better come see me if he wants to play Romeo... and bring us some leftover pies.

ACT ONE

CONDELL: Now there's a good idea.

HEMINGES: Condell, you go to the bakery and I'll see about the parts.

They exit. TOOLEY and BURBAGE have a moment of awkwardness.

TOOLEY: Are you well, Master Burbage, after the first play?

BURBAGE: (*weary*) Very hale. Ready for another, always ready.

TOOLEY: You didn't tell them I was coming. You didn't warn them about my manner, nowadays.

BURBAGE: Aye, well, it's one thing to read of it in a letter, but it's another thing to see it before you. You might be in women's weeds, but you're still one of us, aren't you?

TOOLEY: Let's just see how it goes.

BURBAGE: (*After an awkward pause*) They laugh when it's a comedy, and they cry when it's a tragedy...

TOOLEY: Aye, they do, but they still love Richard Burbage.

BURBAGE: Not all love Burbage as much as they used. You've returned to us at a desperate time. Richard Burbage, the shining light of the Globe playhouse, is having to fight for good roles, and decent players like Heminges and Condell just get the slops.

TOOLEY: There's plenty of good parts in Romeo and Juliet, if they don't give you Romeo.

BURBAGE: My guess is they'll want me for the Apothecary. If so, they can find someone else.

TOOLEY: But that is one of the most important roles.

BURBAGE: He's just an afterthought Will Shakespeare put in to make his play work.

TOOLEY: Nay, he's a Potion Maker of Mantua. We must array you, come.

TOOLEY retrieves a cloak from BURBAGE'S rack, and discovers it is filled with script pages pinned inside. She is a little taken aback, but does not say anything as she helps BURBAGE into the cloak.

BURBAGE: Mrs Burbage will be pleased, very pleased, that you're back. Did I tell you we have another child this winter? That makes... ten, I think.

TOOLEY: Another *grand*child, surely, Burbage?

BURBAGE: (*sudden anger*) Do you know my children better than I?

TOOLEY: (*complete acquiescence*) Nay, Master Burbage.

BURBAGE: (*forgiving*) Mrs Burbage is always better pleased about me being in the playhouse all hours when she knows you are here to see after me.

TOOLEY: Show me how it falls. (*BURBAGE poses for her*) You look very fine.

BURBAGE: Nick?

TOOLEY: Dickie?

BURBAGE: You'll always be here, won't you, when I come off the stage?

TOOLEY: Aye, I will.

BURBAGE opens his arms to her. They kiss, intimately. The sounds of the others approaching down the steps sees them swiftly come apart.

CONDELL: (*entering, with pie basket*) I could add a jig, this fellow could be a musician, always playing a lute for his mistress. Where is my old lute?

HEMINGES: (*entering*) Just stick to the role Condell.

CONDELL: A Fool can always tell a joke or two, and nobody is going to stop him, it's not like I'm on a third-rate part.

HEMINGES: My part is second-rate, and no less. Montague is one of the Lords.

CONDELL: You are playing a mere storytelling device.

ACT ONE

HEMINGES: There is Lord Capulet, Juliet's father, and then there is Lord Montague, Romeo's father, who is every bit as important as Lord Capulet.

CONDELL: Bollocks.

HEMINGES: Condell thinks he's going to add bits here and there to fluff up his part.

CONDELL: You'd do well to fluff up your own part and leave mine well alone.

BURBAGE: Cease your prattling and ready yourselves. Where are those young bucks, come to ask our permission to play the lovers?

HEMINGES: Master Tooley is on near the start. They sent these down for him. (*He passes Lady Montague's headwear to TOOLEY*) They needed someone for old Montague's wife, and I said you'd be perfect.

BURBAGE: Hard luck, but think of it as a way to ease yourself back into playing.

TOOLEY: I did not come back to play.

HEMINGES: Then while you're on the stage, duckie, perchance you work out what it is you did come back for. (*To BURBAGE*) You're the Apothecary, who gives Romeo the poison.

BURBAGE: I know what the infernal Apothecary does!

HEMINGES: Condell is playing Peter, the servant to the nurse.

CONDELL: A servant to a servant! They must cease this habit of giving me all the important roles.

HEMINGES: It's royal robes this afternoon men, not togas. Put your helmets away and find yourself a feathered hat. (*He digs out a hat and cloak*) I'm Lord Montague, so I'll be in some of the big scenes.

TOOLEY: One scene, in truth, and if my pedant's brain serves me, you'll also have a little bit towards the middle.

HEMINGES: Ah, we can rely on you to remind us of our entrances and exits.

TOOLEY: Nay, you cannot call on me when you drop your lines, Master Heminges. I'll take my leave and give my role to one of the boys upstairs.

BURBAGE: Tell one of them he's playing the Apothecary. Burbage will not.

HEMINGES: I'm sure there'll be spare boys willing to go on for you two, only find one that looks and sounds a bit like the great Richard Burbage, because the crowd is expecting to see him. It said so, duckie, on your little piece of paper.

TOOLEY: (*to BURBAGE*) Will you stay and play the Apothecary, if I go on with you?

BURBAGE: Nay... I'll go on for a bigger role, but not that one.

HEMINGES: (*to TOOLEY*) You and I are on as soon as they sound the trumpets. Array yourself!

HEMINGES and CONDELL go to undress, trying to conceal their nakedness.

TOOLEY: Masters, I have seen a man out of his clothes before, and not tried to make him mine, but if you'd be more comfortable hiding your glorious forms, I can wait upstairs.

HEMINGES: Nay, your place is down here with us. We're not going to make a fuss about Master Tooley, now are we? (*CONDELL shakes his head*) Perchance you just sit by the steps and tell me if you can spot any printer's boys in the crowd.

TOOLEY: You're letting printers into the playhouse now?

CONDELL: Much has changed since you were in the playhouse, Master Tooley. They'll have real women playing soon enough.

ACT ONE

BURBAGE: Don't believe him, it will never happen.

CONDELL: And there's never a rehearsal for the bit players, because there's no lines apart from whatever you can drag up from (*taps his head*) within your receptacle.

TOOLEY: It won't be much of a play, without all the lines.

CONDELL: We all know how the stories go, just follow the patterns... you enter, you wait and you listen, then you throw in a line or two which you think sounds right according to your part. Make it a rhyme, if you have the time. Keep it short, or have some sport... it doesn't have to be Shakespeare.

HEMINGES: We don't do too many old plays by Master Shakespeare, not these days, because whenever we do the printers send a pair of their pock-faced boys to sit up the back and scribble down our words as best they can. By the time they go to print with it, Will's best poetry sounds like a madhouse ditty!

TOOLEY: I might have been away from this playhouse for many years, Heminges, but I do recall you once had a grand plan to print all the plays of Master Shakespeares in the one book.

HEMINGES: I did, but then one player of this playhouse took it upon himself to sell the contents of his receptacle to a printer, and when the little books of Master Shakespeares became so popular no printer was interested in paying for our plays anymore, they were only interested in stealing more of them. If I ever discover which player it was I'll hang him by his balls from the top of this playhouse, but I could never catch him at it. I always thought it had to be a player who disappeared from our playhouse (*all eyes fall on TOOLEY*), and never dared show his face back (*cont'd*)

HEMINGES: (*cont'd*) here again.
> *A sudden round of trumpets starts the play. Applause from the crowd.*

CONDELL: We're off!

BURBAGE: No-one is listening to you prattle, Heminges, ready yourself.

HEMINGES: I have, but where is my Lady Montague?
> *TOOLEY puts on his headwear and checks her face in her mirror.*

TOOLEY: Oh dear... I am not ready for this.
> *HEMINGES makes a grand show of taking TOOLEY'S arm in a strong grip.*

HEMINGES: You'll soon be, duckie. A player who does not play has no place in a playhouse!
> *TOOLEY and HEMINGES exit. CONDELL retouches his heavy clown make-up.*

BURBAGE: Did you get a look at what's-his-name while you were up there, the leggy one?

CONDELL: Taylor? Aye, he was drinking with the other shareholders.

BURBAGE: Well, he'll soon show his mettle when he slips up. It's all drinking, whoring, and lording it over the shareholders, until the third day, when his carousing catches up with him. These young players cannot hold their piss the way we can, eh Condell? (*There is another trumpet round*) Come, follow the play for me.

CONDELL: We are not on for a very long time.

BURBAGE: Watch Taylor for me. I'll have to prepare for Romeo in case he slips up.
> *CONDELL shrugs and complies, peering onto the Globe stage, watching the play.*

BURBAGE: (*cont'd*) Who is on?
> *CONDELL cups his hands to his ears, straining.* (*cont'd*)

ACT ONE

(cont'd) BURBAGE furtively digs out a locked box from amongst the mess of his things, takes a key from a chain on his neck, unlocks it, and looks through various pages until he finds the ones he is looking for. He unpins the pages that are inside his cloak and replaces them with the new ones.

BURBAGE: *(cont'd)* Well?

CONDELL: They're just finishing the opening. Here comes Heminges and Tooley.

BURBAGE: How does Tooley look?

CONDELL: Frozen.

BURBAGE: He'll warm up eventually.

CONDELL: Here's Taylor.

BURBAGE: Well, how is he?

CONDELL: Ha! He's got a codpiece as large as a donkey's snout. If he's not careful he'll end up knocking Juliet over with it.

BURBAGE: Nay, it'll be full of nothing but air.

CONDELL: He's doing his best job of mimicking you.

BURBAGE: The crowd probably thinks it is me.

CONDELL: Come now, everybody knows Burbage from Taylor. When they see you, they go into fits of passion. The play stops until they recover.

Applause from upstairs.

BURBAGE: *(introspective)* They laugh when it's a comedy, and they cry when it's a tragedy...

CONDELL: Thanks be that you never tried to play the Fool, or I'd be out of a job.

TOOLEY enters down the steps, in disbelief.

CONDELL: *(cont'd)* Got your taste for the crowd back, Master Tooley?

TOOLEY: I have not been so gazed-upon since I left. It has taken away my breath.

CONDELL: Aye, but it gives you life.

TOOLEY: It does... more than I remember.

BURBAGE: Are you sure Taylor's up to a whole afternoon's work? I could go on for him yet.

TOOLEY: Let me help you on your lines.

BURBAGE: Nay, I have conned them all. I am word-perfect, watch.

BURBAGE stands apart, concealing how he reads lines from inside his cloak.

BURBAGE: (*cont'd*) Romeo calls at my Apothecary rooms, and I say: "Who calls so loud?". Then he goes on a bit about how poor I am, and offers me forty ducats for a dram of poison, then I say: "Such mortal drugs I have; but Mantua's law is death to any he that utters them," and so on. I know my lines, all of them, and I'll feed Romeo his, when he forgets!

HEMINGES enters.

HEMINGES: They're right at the top, centre-back, the little upstarts.

TOOLEY: Who?

HEMINGES: Printer's boys, three of them. I can see their feathers wobbling. There's been two or three 'Romeo and Juliets' stolen by printers over the years. We made a study of their work, as an amusement. How did it go men?

HEMINGES/CONDELL/BURBAGE: "Romeo
Romeo! Wherefore are thou roaming now?
Tell thy father and give up thy name;
Or alone alas I will remain."

HEMINGES: Whatever drivel that springs from our mouths today will be inked as the words of Master William Shakespeare, again.

TOOLEY: (*sarcastically*) If it's so very bad, what are you going to do about it, stop the play?

HEMINGES: There's an idea, we must stop the play.

General shock.

ACT ONE

BURBAGE: We never stop the play!

CONDELL: Bollocks to that, Heminges. We won't get paid.

BURBAGE: If we stop the play we cannot remind the other shareholders what a fine player Master Tooley is.

TOOLEY: I don't know about that. (*Clearing her throat*) I'm not in very good voice.

HEMINGES: Where are we up to?

TOOLEY: (*peering onto the Globe stage*) Capulet's wife and Juliet are not on yet, but soon.

HEMINGES: We should call a halt after that, and push the pies on the crowd, while Condell and I go up and box those printer boys around the ears.

BURBAGE: It is not up to you, Master Heminges, to decide to stop our play. Come, it's time to see to my face. (*He reclines in his chair*) He could be swarthy, this Apothecary, what do you think?

An awkward stand-off occurs when HEMINGES and TOOLEY both go to help BURBAGE make-up his face.

TOOLEY: I always did Master Burbage's face.

HEMINGES: I've done his face for him these ten years.

TOOLEY: Was there no one else to help him?

HEMINGES: Not after you left.

BURBAGE: I need my face done. Tooley, where are you?

TOOLEY: Coming, Master Burbage.

HEMINGES: The face blacking is in that large pot up the back.

TOOLEY: I remember.

HEMINGES: And there is paper underneath for putting it on.

TOOLEY: I see it, thank you Master Heminges.

A defeated HEMINGES retreats to where CONDELL is going over lines in his head.

HEMINGES: (*aside*) Listen, I have been thinking about how to get us back upstairs.

CONDELL: (*aside*) There is no way back upstairs, we've just got to stop down here and play whatever they want us to play.

HEMINGES: The parts will run out soon enough. If I must stop playing, I mean to keep getting my share of the takings.

CONDELL: Look what happened to Shakespeare when he stopped playing. He went to his grave soon enough!

HEMINGES: The only way to retire on the same money is to make ourselves indispensable to this company by doing something other than playing.

CONDELL: What else can a player do?

HEMINGES: What if we dig out Shakespeare's copy of *Romeo and Juliet*? It must be down here somewhere. It's about time we took it to a printer and just kept the coin. All we'd have to do is register it with the Stationers Guild before that printer does. We could take it right now, I'm not on again until the middle of the play.

CONDELL: When the other shareholders find us out, that'll be the end for us. I don't want to go scratching around the bear pits to feed my family. My shares are all I've got, and I'll go on playing for them.

HEMINGES: When the shareholders find us out they'll clamber over one another for a share of the money.

CONDELL: How much?

HEMINGES: For Master Shakespeare's Romeo and Juliet? His original *Romeo and Juliet*, instead of this drivel we are playing today? Condell... it would be like jewels instead of glass beads, like venison instead of rabbit. You know how Shakespeare wrote (*cont'd*)

ACT ONE

HEMINGES: *(cont'd)* the words.

CONDELL: Shakespeare's gone to his grave, and if he didn't register any of his copies with the Stationers', then he's only got himself to blame. Why do you think we were shoved down here with Burbage?

HEMINGES: Because the younger men decided we're too old to run the playhouse.

CONDELL: Nay, it's because we made trouble. Make no mistake, this is the last stop, don't give the shareholders an excuse to show us the door next time.

HEMINGES retreats to look for scripts in the detritus, making a racket, which the others try to ignore. After a moment TOOLEY stops her work and approaches HEMINGES, wiping his fingers on some of the paper. BURBAGE has fallen asleep.

TOOLEY: Perchance you keep it quiet in there Master Heminges? It is supposed to be a serene night in Verona on the stage.

HEMINGES: Never fear, they won't hear me from up there, duckie.

TOOLEY uses a scrap of paper on BURBAGE'S make-up, HEMINGES notices it.

HEMINGES: *(cont'd)* What's that?

TOOLEY: What's what?

HEMINGES: That paper, in your hand?

TOOLEY: You told me to use it on Burbage's face.

HEMINGES takes it. No matter which way he holds it, he can't read it.

HEMINGES: This handwriting is so tight, and so covered in face paint, I cannot unravel it. Read it for me.

TOOLEY/HAMLET: *(reading)* "Tis now the very witching time of night, when churchyards yawn and hell itself breathes out contagion to this world..."

MERELY PLAYERS

BURBAGE/HAMLET: (*waking*) "...now could I drink hot blood, and do such bitter business as the day would quake to look on..." (*laughing*) are we doing *Hamlet* again?

HEMINGES: Is it Shakespeare's lightning hand?

TOOLEY: Small, malformed, letters... aye, it's Will's writing.

HEMINGES: Are there any more of these?

TOOLEY shrugs, and HEMINGES starts to clear things around BURBAGE.

BURBAGE: Heminges, have you forgot yourself?

HEMINGES uncovers a significant pile of papers, handing sections to TOOLEY.

HEMINGES: Read it, quickly.

TOOLEY: A moment...

HEMINGES: Is it the other half of *Hamlet*?

TOOLEY: I think so.

HEMINGES: (*to BURBAGE*) Where have you been throwing the scraps?

BURBAGE: On the floor (*HEMINGES dives for the scraps, collecting them and smoothing them out*), and after that, I take them home, to light my fire.

HEMINGES: Your fire?

BURBAGE: Aye. Mrs Burbage finds it cold at night.

HEMINGES: Your fire has been warming Mrs Burbage with some very fine words.

BURBAGE: Don't you speak ill of Mrs Burbage!

TOOLEY: Here's *Twelfth Night*, and *King Henry*, and underneath... it appears to be *Othello*.

BURBAGE: You call yourself players, but if you can't find your words in your receptacles, then you are not up to the job!

HEMINGES: What more has already gone up in flames? (*Silence*) Answer me Burbage.

ACT ONE

BURBAGE: (*repelling them all*) Nobody said you could come down here, into my private room, sniffing around my things, get off, all of you!

HEMINGES: I have good reason for consulting Will's copy of *Romeo and Juliet*.

BURBAGE: Well, spit it out, we are all shareholders here.

HEMINGES: Is Tooley still a shareholder, after ten years away?

BURBAGE: We are all shareholders, and though I might have closed my eyes for a moment, I thought I heard you say, John Heminges, that you were planning to take our *Romeo and Juliet* to a printer. Why should we give it to you, knowing you intend to do such a thing?

HEMINGES: Nay, it was not what you think. I think there is money to be made, if we players were to talk to a printer ourselves. Good coin, for every man.

BURBAGE: I might have been dreaming, John Heminges, but did I not hear you condemn the player who sold his memory of the plays to a printer?

HEMINGES: I did say it, but this would be different.

BURBAGE: Oh, this would be different?

HEMINGES: Aye, just printing the one play. Romeo and Juliet.

BURBAGE: Heminges, when did you ever read a printed play that was as good as a played one?

HEMINGES: I don't read plays, as a habit.

BURBAGE: Nor do I, and I know Master Tooley never did, and I do believe Master Condell would agree. That makes no man in this room a fool for reading plays. The printers can never ink a play exactly as we play it, just like we players never play it exactly as the writer wrote it.

HEMINGES: (*not following*) Are you saying a (*cont'd*)

HEMINGES: (*cont'd*) player is no better than a printer?

BURBAGE: My brother built this playhouse, from the ground up, and none of it, not one splinter, was ever made with a plan of working with an ink-blood like a printer. Plays do not exist on paper, players, they exist in a player's memory, in a playhouse, and nothing more. A printed play is just an excuse for a man to avoid paying to see a play on the stage, and no player should ever wish that on his company.

HEMINGES: We should have kept a better eye on the copies. Listen to me, all of you, if we want *Romeo and Juliet* to be printed the way Will wrote it, we have got to stop this play.

BURBAGE: You will not stop this play, not when we have Master Tooley back-

HEMINGES: Why all this fuss about Tooley? (*To TOOLEY*) Did Burbage get you back with a promise of unpaid shares?

TOOLEY: Nay, I did not ask it of him.

HEMINGES: Where would the company find the coin to pay Tooley for all those years? We've already spent it!

BURBAGE: You heard what he said, he's not come back for the money.

HEMINGES: What's he come back for then? There won't be too many parts for old women.

BURBAGE: He can play out of the skirts, he's done it before.

TOOLEY: I don't want to play out of the skirts.

BURBAGE: Then no man should get himself worked up.

HEMINGES: Tooley is gone ten years, and he's back not five minutes before I catch him with a piece of play in his hand! Next he'll be running off to a (*cont'd*)

ACT ONE

HEMINGES: (*cont'd*) printing company with the rest of it!

TOOLEY: You always made trouble when you didn't get your way.

HEMINGES: And you always ran off when you didn't get yours.

BURBAGE: Sit down Heminges, you need to go over your part. Tooley, you also. You are Romeo's parents, and you must be ready.

HEMINGES: I am going to stop this play, whether you like it or not.

CONDELL: Not when I am about to go onto the stage.

CONDELL peers onto the Globe stage, checks on progress, retrieves his hat and moves for the steps. HEMINGES goes to stop him, but BURBAGE holds him back.

BURBAGE: Quickly Condell, get up there!

CONDELL manages to get up the stairs. HEMINGES gets himself free of BURBAGE by pushing him aside.

BURBAGE: (*cont'd*) Tooley, block the stairs!

TOOLEY tries her best to get in the way, holding up her fists. HEMINGES easily pushes TOOLEY aside and goes to ascend, but BURBAGE leaps onto his back and covers HEMINGES' face.

BURBAGE: Block the way!

TOOLEY: Nay, not while he's thrashing.

BURBAGE: Nicholas Tooley, I command you to block the way!

TOOLEY: You command me?

BURBAGE: I am your Master! I still have your apprentice papers, signed and sealed, I command you!

TOOLEY is torn between loyalty and fear, and reluctantly blocks HEMINGES from ascending the stairs. BURBAGE manages to hold HEMINGES' arms.

BURBAGE: *(cont'd)* Heminges, sit down to a rehearsal with Master Tooley.

HEMINGES: You were never my master, Burbage.

BURBAGE realises he's at the right height to see onto the Globe stage from HEMINGES' back.

BURBAGE: Quiet... he starts... *(he recites what he sees onstage)* "Knock, knock, knock! Who's there, i' the name of Beelzebub? Here's a farmer, that hanged himself on the expectation of plenty..." Then more knocking within... "Knock, knock! Who's there-" What was Shakespeare thinking with all that "knock-knock", is it supposed to be funny?

HEMINGES: Is that from *Romeo and Juliet*?

BURBAGE: Of course it's not from *Romeo and Juliet*. It's the light relief, after Macbeth has murdered the King. I never saw it, of course, because I was washing the blood off. Knock-knock! Who's there? It's terrible, it'll never make anyone laugh.

A great round of laughter and applause goes up. HEMINGES walks down the steps.

BURBAGE: *(cont'd)* Take me back, I want to see it.

HEMINGES: Condell, you're a genius! Look for the printer's boys, are they scribbling?

TOOLEY: Aye, like mad.

HEMINGES: Excellent work, Condell.

TOOLEY: He's exiting. He'll be here in a moment.

CONDELL enters down the steps. HEMINGES lowers BURBAGE off his back.

HEMINGES: You had me fooled, here I was thinking you weren't behind me, but all the time you were! Every one of us could do what Condell has done and play any old lines to the printer's boys. Their new Romeo and Juliet will be worse than all the others put together. I might do some of my old lines from *(cont'd)*

ACT ONE

HEMINGES: *(cont'd)* *Julius Caesar*, what say you, Condell?

CONDELL: I fancied I'd fit every clown I ever played into this *Romeo and Juliet*. What do you wager I can't manage it?

BURBAGE: Enough. Sit down, and keep it quiet. I can see you men are going to play this like little boys. No player is to go off his part again. I am going up to speak to the other shareholders.

HEMINGES: Nay, Burbage, I'll go.

BURBAGE: I am the senior shareholder, I am the one to speak to them.

HEMINGES: Tell them that our play is being stolen, again.

BURBAGE: I'll not be asking them to stop the play, get that idea out of your receptacle. What we need is a meeting of every man, in the alehouse after the play is over, to speak of shares, and our new season, now that Master Tooley has returned to us. If you can find anyone who is interested, you can raise your point about the printer's boys then.

HEMINGES: Are you going to tell them about how Tooley arrays himself?

BURBAGE: What do you mean?

HEMINGES: You know what I mean. Is Tooley to come to the alehouse dressed like that?

BURBAGE: Of course he won't. He'll have removed all the Montague woman's weeds before.

HEMINGES: What about what's under the Montague woman's weeds?

BURBAGE: Tooley's under the Montague woman's weeds. They'll just have to grow familiar with the weeds.

HEMINGES: Let me come with you, I'll help you *(cont'd)*

HEMINGES: *(cont'd)* with the stairs.

BURBAGE: Nay, you will stay down here, all of you. Have something to eat.

> *BURBAGE exits up the steps. CONDELL hands the pie basket around. HEMINGES takes one, undoes the paper wrapping and uses it to wipe his mouth as he eats.*

HEMINGES: One of us should have gone with him.

TOOLEY: You mean to say you should have gone with him.

HEMINGES: I am only trying to help all of us.

TOOLEY: There is one thing that has not changed in all the years I was away.

HEMINGES: Where were you these many seasons?

TOOLEY: You probably never noticed how much it pained me, to sit and watch you all on the stage, with the younger boys playing in my old finery.

HEMINGES: Now I remember, there was that problem with the new boy player.

TOOLEY: The problem was not with the boy, the problem was with the mother.

HEMINGES: It's worse now, we cannot have a hint of sodomy about the playhouse.

TOOLEY: I never touched him.

HEMINGES: They'll shut us down if they think we're harbouring sodomites.

TOOLEY: Sometimes, the new boys took it badly when I showed them how to strap themselves down, in between their legs, but that little shyte said something about it to its mama. She cried like a Puritan, calling sodomy at what she did not understand.

CONDELL: But something must have made you leave, Tooley.

TOOLEY: Cleopatra was the last role Shakespeare wrote for me. I stayed for a season after that, and I *(cont'd)*

ACT ONE

TOOLEY: *(cont'd)* tried playing out of the skirts, but I found that I could not. I took myself away. I admit I saw some very black days. Eventually I was taken in by the good women at the Convent of Saint Helen, and they saved me from the very worst.

HEMINGES: I stopped sending your coin, after the nuns sent it back. We all agreed that meant you must have gone to your grave.

TOOLEY: In a way, I had.

HEMINGES: Well, you'll just have to muck-in as best you can, until all the shareholders have decided what coin there will be for you.

TOOLEY: I will take no coin when I haven't played for it.

HEMINGES: You might have to stick to that plan, Tooley. Paying full shares for old men playing just one or two roles is the fastest way to drive a company of players into the ground.

CONDELL: That's the way it was when old Master Armin was still with us. I played all the big roles, and he did the small, but we got paid the same. It was like that until we had to carry him off the stage to his last bed, and that's the way it's going to be until they come down here and carry me to mine.

HEMINGES: Even a fool could see there are too many shareholders already.

CONDELL: Are you calling me a fool, on the stage, and off?

HEMINGES: Aye, if you cannot see that more shareholders means less money for all of us.

CONDELL: Master Heminges' habit of calling other players fools is what got us down here.

HEMINGES: When this playhouse needed new players, I only pointed out that no young player who *(cont'd)*

MERELY PLAYERS

HEMINGES: (*cont'd*) thought anything of himself would become a shareholder of the Globe playhouse, when all we older players were kept on, unless we gave them something else to make them feel important. I suggested they be allowed to attire themselves closer to the stage. It was a brilliant idea.

CONDELL: So brilliant they moved Burbage down here a month later, with us following this season.

HEMINGES: You might think there is no way back upstairs, Condell, but I do.

An awkward silence. CONDELL and HEMINGES both eat pies.

TOOLEY: Is Master Burbage quite well?

HEMINGES: Aye, you've seen him.

TOOLEY: But on the stage, he is like he always was?

CONDELL: He always makes a big show of handing over his role to one of the younger men, then he swears he's not going on in the small part they give him. We just play along with it, because when it comes to it, he goes on, and he sends the crowd into a passion in even the smallest part. You could get your taste for it again. If any of the boys cannot go on, you can stand in.

HEMINGES: Join us, forever waiting for one of the lads to come down with the French Pox and give us an afternoon's work.

CONDELL finishes off his pie, wipes his mouth, and as he draws the pie wrapping away, HEMINGES notices there is writing on it and grabs it.

HEMINGES: What's here? I can't read it.

CONDELL: (*laughing*) You're seeing Shakespeare's hand everywhere now Heminges.

HEMINGES: Read it!

CONDELL: (*reading*) "Alack, 'tis he: why, he was (*cont'd*)

ACT ONE

CONDELL: *(cont'd)* met even now. As mad as the vex'd sea; singing aloud; Crown'd with rank fumiter and furrow-weeds..."

TOOLEY: "With bur-docks, hemlock, nettles, cuckoo-flowers, darnel, and all the idle weeds that grow in our sustaining corn..." it is from *King Lear*, the daughter, Cordelia.

HEMINGES: Are there more? *(They start unwrapping pies of script sheets)* Is it all the same hand?

CONDELL: Aye, it's Will's.

HEMINGES: Condell, get to the bakery, see what is left.

CONDELL: I'll go when the play is over.

HEMINGES: You'll go now, before they sell more pies wrapped in *King Lear*. None of us is needed on the stage. Get to the bakery and bring all the paper you can find up there.

CONDELL shrugs and exits up the steps.

HEMINGES: *(cont'd)* Gather everything off the floor, every scrap, however small.

TOOLEY and HEMINGES start to sort out the plays.

TOOLEY: I fear my coming back has got you all dancing around like rabbits.

HEMINGES: We haven't had so much to dance about of late. *(Reading)* This looks like *Julius Caesar*, do you have more of *Julius Caesar*?

TOOLEY: This pile here is all Caesar. *(Placing plays together)* Is it also my women's weeds?

HEMINGES: Why would any player think less of another player attired in women's weeds?

TOOLEY: Because I won't be taking them off, when I leave here tonight.

HEMINGES: But you are the same Tooley as was. *(Reading)* Can you make this out?

TOOLEY: *(Reading)* It's from The Dream. I'm not *(cont'd)*

TOOLEY: *(cont'd)* entirely the same.

HEMINGES: You are still a man, when it comes to it, I suppose we can prove that, if the Puritans make a fuss about you. *(Reading)* Here's more bits of *Hamlet*. They're torn but you can make out the words.

TOOLEY: You need not think of me that way, Heminges. I passed for a woman to the nuns.

HEMINGES: *(reading)* More of *Hamlet*, I think.

TOOLEY: A woman knows when a man is not listening to what she is saying.

HEMINGES: Aye, you're sounding more like Mrs Heminges, the more you prattle.

TOOLEY: Then you'll get used to me, in time.

HEMINGES: I remember when you first came to the playhouse, and you were a boy, like every other. The women's weeds were only for the stage. Why did you change?

TOOLEY: What are those pages at your feet?

HEMINGES: *(reading with difficulty)* "O, then, I see Queen Mab hath been with you. She is the fairies' midwife..." it's more fairies from The Dream.

TOOLEY: You are not the same as you were in those days.

HEMINGES: Aha! It's not The Dream, I played him once, it's Mercutio from *Romeo and Juliet*!

TOOLEY: You've grown to be less sure of yourself, and you find it harder to read the roles.

HEMINGES: Bollocks. We might all be changed men, but none has changed as much as you. Only one page of *Romeo and Juliet*? Well, it's a start, there will be more in here, and I'll find it.

CONDELL comes down the steps, a pile of papers in his hand.

CONDELL: Saved, saved from the greasy fingers *(cont'd)*

ACT ONE

CONDELL: *(cont'd)* of bakers' tarts. They had all this stashed in the corner holding up a butter churn, and when I asked if there was more, they stared and blinked at me, as though I was a horse who'd thought to start speaking. One of them piped up and said that they "could nawt rememba whan the paypers cayme". Top of the pile is a slice of Will's Tempest! When I took these from their greasy little fingers, the chatty one had the hide to ask me if I was "gaarn to brang some back to wrap tamorraw's poyes!"

HEMINGES: Tooley, see if there is anything of Romeo and Juliet in there.

TOOLEY looks through the pile.

CONDELL: Tomorrow's pies! She wanted to wrap tomorrow's pies in the only copy of Will Shakespeare's Tempest!

HEMINGES: Perchance you both see our problem better now?

CONDELL: Aye, although I admit I always thought Will Shakespeare's plays were a little overcooked.

TOOLEY: It's most of *The Tempest*, the rest is *As You Like It* and *Antony and Cleopatra*, and something else...

HEMINGES: Read it.

TOOLEY: "If we say that we have no sin, we deceive ourselves, and there is no truth in us. Why, then, belike we must sin, and so consequently die: Ay, we must die an everlasting death. What doctrine call you this, Che sera, sera, What will be, shall be? Divinity, adieu!"

HEMINGES/CONDELL/TOOLEY: Christopher Marlowe.

HEMINGES: Give that rubbish back to the baker's tarts... or even better, write on the back of it. We need some paper, but we'll also need some ink.

TOOLEY: What for?

HEMINGES: When Burbage comes back, we've got to sit him down and get him remembering Romeo's big speeches. You can write them on the back of Marlowe.

TOOLEY: Don't vex Burbage before he goes on as the Apothecary. Wait until the play is over, when he's gathered his wits.

HEMINGES: That will be too late. I only want a handful of pages from *Romeo and Juliet* to take to the Stationers Guild. It's in Burbage's head and I want to get it out. Perchance you want to spend the time on some other matter, Tooley? If the company is going to honour your shares, we could see this as your way of earning them. Fetch some inks.

TOOLEY: I have no interest in my shares, Heminges.

HEMINGES: All we have heard from you today, Tooley, are the many reasons you're not here. You're not here to play, yet you're playing. You're not here to reclaim your shares, yet you've allowed Burbage to go and make representations to the other shareholders on your behalf. While you're working out why you are here, I am asking you to act as scribe for a pressing matter which I believe will be of benefit to the older men in our company. If that is so very objectionable to you, duckie, I think it's time for you to be on your way.

TOOLEY: Alright. I'll scribe for you, but just a few of his big speeches, and you'll go easy.

CONDELL: Aye, I was still hoping we'd get to the alehouse early.

HEMINGES: You can sit and start scribing what they're playing on the stage, while the rest of us go back and remember what's been played so far. Where is *(cont'd)*

ACT ONE

HEMINGES: *(cont'd)* Burbage? We need him back down here, and we need to find some ink in this mess.

TOOLEY: Master Burbage always keeps bottled blood, if I recall.

HEMINGES: It will do.

TOOLEY: I'll craft some quills.

HEMINGES: My thanks to you, Master Tooley.

TOOLEY pulls feathers from HEMINGES' hat and cuts two quills, making herself ready with a makeshift tablet. HEMINGES retrieves a bottle of blood from BURBAGE'S make-up and makes two portions, one for CONDELL and one for TOOLEY. CONDELL sets himself up with a view of the stage and begins scribing. BURBAGE returns quietly down the steps.

HEMINGES: What did the shareholders say?

BURBAGE: Shareholders?

HEMINGES: Will they meet with us today?

BURBAGE: They laugh when it's a comedy, and they cry when it's a tragedy...

HEMINGES: Aye, that's what brings in the money. What did they say Burbage?

CONDELL: *(aside)* He didn't do it.

HEMINGES: *(aside)* Methinks he had not the audience he wanted.

CONDELL: *(aside)* Doesn't want to admit it.

BURBAGE: Where are we up to?

CONDELL: *(peering onto the Globe stage)* Juliet's father is speaking with her, very sternly.

HEMINGES: Burbage, I want you to recite all Romeo's big speeches. Tooley will scribe for you.

BURBAGE: I know all my big speeches, I don't need them written down.

HEMINGES: The balcony scene would be a very good start.

BURBAGE: You want me to say it, without anyone here to see it?

HEMINGES: Here's your chance to play Romeo this afternoon, old man.

BURBAGE: I think perchance you are addled in your head. I only say the play when there is a crowd before me, and they've paid their pennies to see it.

HEMINGES: Aye, that's what we usually do, but today we need to do something a little out of the ordinary.

BURBAGE: Why?

HEMINGES: Because *Romeo and Juliet* is being stolen, again, and Will's copy seems to have gone up in flames in Mrs Burbage's parlour fire, or been cooked in the Globe playhouse bakery!

BURBAGE: It's all in here (*taps the side of his head*) in my receptacle. It cannot be stolen.

HEMINGES: Aye, that's what we all believed, until today, yet stolen this play will be if we let it finish and we do nothing. Just regale us with a little of your memory, Burbage.

BURBAGE: My memory?

HEMINGES: Aye, remind us what a good play Romeo and Juliet was.

TOOLEY: Start with the balcony scene.

BURBAGE: Balcony?

TOOLEY: I'm up top, but I don't see you climb up.

BURBAGE/ROMEO: (*gearing-up*) Oh aye... aye... "But, soft! what light through yonder window breaks?"

TOOLEY: That's it.

BURBAGE/ROMEO: "It is the east, and Juliet is the sun. Arise, fair sun, and kill the envious moon, Who is..." (*he dries*)

HEMINGES: Run at it again, straight away.

BURBAGE/ROMEO: "But, soft! what light (*cont'd*)

ACT ONE

BURBAGE/ROMEO: *(cont'd)* through yonder window breaks? It is the east, and Juliet is the sun. Arise, fair sun, and kill the envious moon."

BURBAGE looks very pleased with himself.

TOOLEY: Now, the rest. (*BURBAGE is crestfallen*) A pause, I think.

HEMINGES: A pause, after only... three lines?

TOOLEY: Aye, a moment.

HEMINGES: Alright, but we must get on with it.

TOOLEY helps BURBAGE into his chair and helps him prepare the lines. HEMINGES goes to CONDELL'S side, scribing the play on the Globe stage.

HEMINGES: *(cont'd)* Are you getting it down?

CONDELL: Aye, in bits.

HEMINGES: Show me.

CONDELL: Get me a drink first, it'll flow better with something inside me.

HEMINGES: *(He pours CONDELL a drink)* Let me see it.

CONDELL hands over a page. HEMINGES pores over it.

HEMINGES: *(cont'd)* Is that the best you can do?

CONDELL: What's wrong with it?

HEMINGES: Well, it's hard to follow.

CONDELL: That'll be your bad eyes.

HEMINGES: There's nothing wrong with my eyes. Why are you writing it across the page?

CONDELL: To fit it all in.

HEMINGES: Write down the page, and put every character's name in large letters, so it can be seen. Are you putting in the pauses and the gestures?

CONDELL: No.

HEMINGES: Well, catch them, otherwise the poetry won't come across.

CONDELL: If you want poetry, you'll have to *(cont'd)*

CONDELL: (*cont'd*) pay a scribe.

HEMINGES: Just do it better. (*To TOOLEY*) Come, get him back, we must press on.

TOOLEY: Ready now... run at it, then all the way through. Juliet is up there, waiting for you, though she does not see you, her Romeo.

BURBAGE/ROMEO: (*rushing it*) "But, soft! what light through yonder window breaks? It is the east, and Juliet is the sun. Arise, fair sun, and kill the envious moon," (*he dries*) "Who is..."

CONDELL: He doesn't have it.

BURBAGE/ROMEO: I have it! "But, soft! what light through yonder window breaks? It is the east, and Juliet is the sun. Arise..." (*he dries*) Why will anyone want to read it?

TOOLEY: Dickie...

BURBAGE: None will want to read it!

CONDELL: He doesn't have it.

BURBAGE: Silence!

TOOLEY leads BURBAGE to his chair. HEMINGES comes to CONDELL'S side.

HEMINGES: (*aside*) You know what it's like when it doesn't flow and every man can see it.

CONDELL: (*aside*) Aye, but his well seems to have run completely dry!

HEMINGES: He can still do it. They haven't taken him off the stage, they wouldn't dare!

CONDELL: He is getting much lesser roles now. It matters not if he prattles bits of this and that, he knows what carriage to put behind it. Then you come along and ask him to say Romeo's words, but he cannot remember more than three lines! Take my advice, Heminges, just leave all this and let's go to the alehouse early...

ACT ONE

HEMINGES: Nay, not until we have enough to show the Stationers'. (*To TOOLEY*) Tooley, you realise what we are trying to do here?

TOOLEY: (*coming over*) I do, but you're going about it in the wrong way.

HEMINGES: Oh?

TOOLEY: You cannot throw a man into the middle of a play, and expect him to find his way. A play is not for carrying by one man only. Feed it into him, and that will draw him out.

HEMINGES: Ah-ha, yes. You see Condell, we only have to draw him out. Come, what is the scene?

TOOLEY: Capulet's orchard.

HEMINGES: Write that down. Now, what do we see?

TOOLEY: Juliet is on the balcony.

HEMINGES: Aha, yes. Write that in too. We need a Juliet (*he realises it must be him*). Both of you, keep writing. I'll be the Juliet.

HEMINGES makes a makeshift balcony from props baskets and stands on it.

TOOLEY: You're but four and ten years old, arrayed by your Mother.

HEMINGES: Assume I am in the garments. The age you'll just have to forgive. What am I doing?

TOOLEY: You've just met Romeo for the first time.

HEMINGES: Ah, that's you Burbage. I've met you and I have fallen for you.

BURBAGE: Ha!

TOOLEY: She's not fallen, not yet. She's only... thinking about him at this point.

HEMINGES: (*impersonating*) Aye, I'm thinking about my Romeo.

TOOLEY: She is supposed to be so beautiful that the moon would be envious to shine upon her.

HEMINGES: Well, use your imagination. Come, my Romeo.

BURBAGE/ROMEO: "But, soft! what light through yonder window breaks? It is the east, and Juliet is the sun. Arise, fair sun, and kill the envious moon, Who is already sick and pale with grief, that thou her maid art far more fair than she..." (*dries*)

HEMINGES: Did you get it?

TOOLEY: (*writing*) Aye.

HEMINGES: You were right, he remembered more of it. Try again, Burbage.

BURBAGE/HAMLET: "Angels and ministers of grace defend us! Be thou a spirit of health or goblin damn'd, bring with thee airs from heaven or blasts from hell, be thy intents wicked or charitable..."

HEMINGES and TOOLEY look to one another, TOOLEY shakes his head.

HEMINGES: That's not Romeo, is it?

BURBAGE/HAMLET: "I'll call thee Hamlet, King, father, royal Dane: O, answer me! Let me not burst in ignorance; but tell..."

HEMINGES: You have the wrong play, Burbage, we need Romeo.

BURBAGE: Go and see Master Shakespeare, and ask him to give you the words.

TOOLEY, HEMINGES and CONDELL are all shocked.

HEMINGES: But, Master Shakespeare is gone to his grave.

BURBAGE: Nay, Master Shakespeare's gone to the country to write me another play.

HEMINGES: Burbage, you know very well that Shakespeare has been dead these three years.

BURBAGE: He's going to write me a role for an (*cont'd*)

ACT ONE

BURBAGE: (*cont'd*) old foolish King, who spoils with his children.

HEMINGES: That was *King Lear*. It is already written.

BURBAGE: Will's only stalling for time. Meanwhile, we're to put together a season. Master Tooley is returned, and we'll get all the Lord Chamberlain's Men back to the playhouse now.

HEMINGES: They haven't called us the Lord Chamberlain's Men these many years, not since the Queen went to her grave. We are the King's Men now, remember?

HEMINGES retrieves the pages of King Lear and shows BURBAGE.

HEMINGES: (*cont'd*) Here is *King Lear*, already on the page, and already played on the stage.

TOOLEY: You were the King in that one Dickie.

BURBAGE: I was?

TOOLEY: You were a fine King. It was long ago now.

BURBAGE: They laugh when it's a comedy, and they cry when it's a tragedy...

TOOLEY: Aye, come and lie yourself down.

TOOLEY leads BURBAGE to his chair.

CONDELL: (*aside*) He is past it, Heminges. No more.

HEMINGES: (*aside*) Nay, you saw him, Hamlet was flowing out of him like a spring!

TOOLEY: (*aside*) Burbage must restore himself before he goes onto the stage. Where are we up to?

CONDELL: (*peering onto Globe stage*) Tybalt's just knifed Mercutio.

TOOLEY: Oh, we've been wasting our time. We are on again soon Heminges.

HEMINGES: We only need a little more of the balcony scene. Between that and what Condell has scribbled, and whatever's left of Will's copies, we'll have a (*cont'd*)

MERELY PLAYERS

HEMINGES: (*cont'd*) good chunk to make our claim with the Stationers Guild.

TOOLEY: (*Checking her face in her mirror*) What claim?

HEMINGES: We'll have to move quickly on to the rest of Will's plays. All the words must go to a printer, and now, if Burbage's state is what it seems. Every printer in London would be happy to get his hands on the complete works of William Shakespeare, we could command a top price.

TOOLEY: Wait until we come off, and I'll assist you with Burbage. He needs a soft touch.

HEMINGES: We have time yet. Get Burbage up and get him remembering.

TOOLEY: (*to CONDELL*) Remind Master Heminges that there are penalties for players who are late for their cues.

TOOLEY checks the Globe stage, and touches up her make-up.

CONDELL: You heard him.

TOOLEY: (*to CONDELL*) Inform him that Nicholas Tooley, shareholder of the King's Men, will make application for ten years' unpaid shares, if he comes off to find that Master Heminges has taken steps in his grand plan to force any more words out of Master Burbage.

TOOLEY exits up the steps.

HEMINGES: (*shouting after her*) I knew you'd come back because you wanted something!

CONDELL: He's got you by the bollocks. You may as well just go on, and then, the alehouse.

HEMINGES approaches BURBAGE and wakes him.

BURBAGE: Am I on?

HEMINGES: Aye, Burbage. We're doing Romeo, and you've just seen Juliet.

ACT ONE

BURBAGE: "Be thou a spirit of health or goblin damn'd…"

HEMINGES: No, we don't want a ghost, we want Romeo.

CONDELL: Heminges, go easy.

HEMINGES: You just keep writing. Burbage, Juliet is on the balcony, you remember.

HEMINGES stands BURBAGE on the spot, then collects the scribing tools.

BURBAGE: Remember… remember? Aye, "Remember thee! Ay, thou poor ghost, while memory holds a seat in this distracted globe. Remember thee!"

HEMINGES: (*to CONDELL*) Is that Romeo? (*CONDELL shrugs*).

BURBAGE: "I'll wipe away all trivial fond records
All saws of books, all forms, all pressures past,
That youth and observation copied there;
And thy commandment all alone shall live
Within the book and volume of my brain…"

HEMINGES: Burbage, is that from *Romeo and Juliet*?

BURBAGE: You would do well to ask Will Shakespeare.

HEMINGES: Nay, Burbage, you can remember!

BURBAGE: "Remember thee! Ay, thou poor ghost, while memory holds a seat in this distracted globe…" (*he dries*)

HEMINGES: Listen to me Burbage. The people out there, they want Shakespeare's words, the crowd is waiting for Romeo.

CONDELL: Heminges, you are needed on the stage.

HEMINGES: They can wait.

BURBAGE: They laugh when it's a comedy, and they cry when it's a tragedy…

HEMINGES: (*to BURBAGE*) I can see into your head, old man, and I know you are only acting like (*cont'd*)

HEMINGES: (*cont'd*) you cannot remember, but I want you to remember, for all our sakes. Remember!

CONDELL: (*pulling HEMINGES away*) Leave off!

HEMINGES: (*shaking BURBAGE violently*) You just don't want to remember!

BURBAGE falls heavily, hits his head on the floor and passes out cold. CONDELL goes to rouse BURBAGE, but he cannot.

CONDELL: That was a bad fall. Burbage! (*To HEMINGES*) He will tell Tooley what you did.

HEMINGES: Nay, he'll not remember what happened!

CONDELL: (*joking*) I think you've killed him. Help me get him up.

HEMINGES: I've wanted to knock some sense into the old bastard for years.

CONDELL: Come, I'll lift his head and you get the legs.

HEMINGES: I need to go to the stage.

CONDELL discovers the play pages pinned inside BURBAGE'S cloak. He laughs.

CONDELL: You owe me a crown, Heminges. I know how the old man remembers all his lines.

HEMINGES: What?

CONDELL: He's got play pages in his cloak. Printer's pages, by the looks.

HEMINGES: Printer's pages?

CONDELL: (*to BURBAGE*) I can see how you're word-perfect now, Master Burbage.

CONDELL tries to rouse BURBAGE, who remains lifeless.

CONDELL: (*cont'd*) I think you have really killed him.

HEMINGES: Bollocks, he's only playing. All day, he's just been playing with me.

CONDELL: (*Noticing something on his hand*) Oh, there's blood. I need something to clean him up.

ACT ONE

CONDELL spies the plays sitting nearby, and HEMINGES reads his mind.

HEMINGES: Nay, do not use those!

CONDELL: You can say farewell to Shakespeare now, Heminges, Burbage is dead, pass me the papers, there is more blood coming!

HEMINGES spooks, grabs his hat, and exits up the stairs, leaving CONDELL to contemplate the devastation.

Act Two

As before, beneath the stage of London's Globe Theatre. CONDELL paces, watching the action on the Globe stage. BURBAGE lies covered by bloodstained play pages. After a moment, TOOLEY and HEMINGES come down the stairs. There is tension in the air.

HEMINGES: None would believe it's ten years since you were on the stage, Tooley, you played that very well.
TOOLEY: Where is Burbage? It's nearly time for him to go on.
HEMINGES: Burbage? Aye, Condell, you saw him last, where is Burbage?
CONDELL: Don't make me say it.
TOOLEY: Say what?
CONDELL: He's had a little... spill.
TOOLEY: What?
CONDELL: They were going at each other, he... *(pointing at HEMINGES)* he was going at Burbage, and...
TOOLEY: Oh, was he?
CONDELL: Aye, wanting Burbage to remember the play.
TOOLEY: Where is Burbage now?
CONDELL: I have to go on.
TOOLEY: Where is he?
   CONDELL points to the pile of papers, then disappears up the stairs to the Globe stage.
TOOLEY: *(cont'd)* Let's get you into your chair Burbage.
   TOOLEY lifts the bloodstained pages from BURBAGE'S head and shoulders, then draws back, letting out a cry.
TOOLEY: *(cont'd)* What have you done?

HEMINGES: I was only trying to get him to see sense.
TOOLEY: What?
HEMINGES: He wouldn't remember his lines.
TOOLEY: But there is so much blood...
HEMINGES: I did not mean to knock him.
TOOLEY: Knock him? Knock him with what?
HEMINGES: I meant shake him... I didn't mean to shake him.
TOOLEY: You shook him? A frail old man, and you shook him?
HEMINGES: He just fell over. I didn't mean for him to die.
TOOLEY: He's supposed to play the Apothecary, and soon.
HEMINGES: I know it.
TOOLEY: You were hoping to stop the play.
HEMINGES: Not like this.
TOOLEY: I know you to be a man who likes to see his will done, Heminges, but this is a dark path to getting your way.
HEMINGES: Nay, think not that of me Tooley. I did not mean to kill him, I swear it.
TOOLEY: Dear God, think of what we'll have to say to Mrs Burbage! She will not bear this, Heminges. (*Collapsing in grief*) Oh Dickie, not like this.
HEMINGES: We could just say he keeled over.
TOOLEY: You will tell her the truth!
HEMINGES: Such an old man should not spend his days around the playhouse.
TOOLEY: I should never have left. This would never have happened if I hadn't left.
HEMINGES: Don't blame yourself, Tooley, he was on his last legs.
TOOLEY: I don't blame myself, it is just the latest (*cont'd*)

ACT TWO

TOOLEY: *(cont'd)* tragedy in the management of this playhouse by Master John Heminges, who never listens to the other men, and must always see his will done.

HEMINGES: Manager of the King's Men? Me? Oh duckie, our manager lies dead before you. Burbage never let me manage anything.

TOOLEY: You always tried your best to undermine him, and you managed to get rid of me.

HEMINGES: You left, I never pushed you.

TOOLEY: I was Burbage's apprentice. I could have managed him, and I could have managed this playhouse better than you.

HEMINGES: So you're back to claim your rightful place, is that it?

TOOLEY: Help me get his costume off.

HEMINGES: What?

TOOLEY: Get the cloak, and the hat. You're going on as the Apothecary.

HEMINGES: I don't know the lines.

TOOLEY: They're inside the cloak

HEMINGES and TOOLEY manage to lift BURBAGE up and get the cloak from him. HEMINGES inspects the pages inside it.

HEMINGES: How long has he been reading his lines from his armpits?

HEMINGES lets BURBAGE fall back.

TOOLEY: Be careful!

HEMINGES: Well, he can't feel it.

TOOLEY: Take the hat, and get ready.

HEMINGES: Where are we up to?

TOOLEY peers through the gap near the stairs.

HEMINGES: *(cont'd)* Help me with the cloak.

TOOLEY: There is still some time.

HEMINGES: Tooley. You must not think ill of me-

TOOLEY: It does not matter what I think of you.

CONDELL enters down the steps.

CONDELL: Are we going on?

TOOLEY: Of course we are going on. Heminges will play the Apothecary.

HEMINGES: (*showing the pages in his cloak*) I've got the lines.

CONDELL: He's on soon, very soon.

HEMINGES/TOOLEY: I know / He knows.

TOOLEY: (*to CONDELL*) Tell me what happened. Heminges told me he knocked Burbage.

HEMINGES: I didn't knock him, he knocked his head when he fell.

TOOLEY: Because you shook him. (*To CONDELL*) Is that what happened?

CONDELL: I was watching the stage, scribing the play.

TOOLEY: If you'd only waited for me to come off you could have had all the words you wanted.

HEMINGES: It doesn't matter now, just wait until I come off before you tell anyone.

TOOLEY: Now he wants to wait.

HEMINGES: So I can make a proper account of what happened.

CONDELL: Aye, perchance old Burbage's time was just up?

TOOLEY: (*going to BURBAGE'S side*) He should not have gone this way. He should have gone to his grave from his own bed.

HEMINGES: He was ailing ever since the winter.

BURBAGE coughs, sending a few bloodied pages into the air. HEMINGES spooks.

TOOLEY: Dickie?

BURBAGE: Where are we up to?

ACT TWO

TOOLEY: Oh, Dickie (*to HEMINGES*) Help me get him up.

They clear away the bloody pages and sit BURBAGE up. TOOLEY mops the blood from his face.

BURBAGE: Am I on yet?

TOOLEY: You've had a fall.

BURBAGE: Who are you?

TOOLEY: It is I, Tooley.

BURBAGE: Tooley? Nay, Tooley is a boy, not an old lady.

TOOLEY: Nick, I am your Nick, who was your apprentice.

BURBAGE: Nay, my Nick Tooley left the playhouse many years ago. Who's that one?

TOOLEY: Master Heminges.

BURBAGE: Heminges? Nay, this crag of a face cannot be young Master Heminges. Am I on yet?

CONDELL: Just rest yourself for a moment.

BURBAGE: (*pointing to CONDELL*) Who is that one?

TOOLEY: It is Henry Condell, just come from the stage.

CONDELL: Heaven and hell! Burbage, we thought you were dead.

BURBAGE: I am perfectly well.

CONDELL: Were you playing with me?

BURBAGE: Playing?

CONDELL: (*emotional*) Aye, were you playing dead with me?

HEMINGES draws TOOLEY and CONDELL aside into rushed conversation.

HEMINGES: He is too frail to do it, I'll go on.

CONDELL: He was dead when you left for the stage.

TOOLEY: He's not that frail, he can do it himself.

HEMINGES: Just now you were saying he's a "poor, frail old man!"

CONDELL: You shook him, and he fell, and he was out cold!

TOOLEY: Luckily for you he's made of sterner stuff than we knew.

HEMINGES: If he goes up there and swoons again it will not be my fault.

CONDELL: You'd best get him ready, he's on very soon.

HEMINGES/TOOLEY: We know!

BURBAGE: I cannot lie here talking to a washer woman and old men, I must ready myself.

TOOLEY: (*to CONDELL*) Go up and tell them to pad it out.

CONDELL exits up the stairs. BURBAGE tries to get himself up. HEMINGES spies the near empty blood bottle underneath him.

HEMINGES: This is where all the blood is from.

TOOLEY: What?

BURBAGE: It's pig's blood, fresh from the tannery by the river.

HEMINGES: (*relieved*) Aha, only pig's blood?

BURBAGE: Aye, they save me the best for my make-up.

HEMINGES and TOOLEY help BURBAGE to his chair.

HEMINGES: (*relieved*) You took a little tumble, is all. You must have knocked over the bottle Tooley was using to write with. That's it, that's what happened.

BURBAGE: Why were you writing with my bottle of pig's blood? You'll have to pay me for it.

TOOLEY: You'll have to ask Master Heminges that later. We've got to get you ready. (*Aside to HEMINGES*) If you meant to stop this play by rendering Master Burbage incapable, then I am happy to report you will fail. Left to his own devices, he might be artless, but in the company of other players, he will (*cont'd*)

ACT TWO

TOOLEY: (*cont'd*) come to life yet.

BURBAGE: Who am I?

TOOLEY: You are Richard Burbage, player of...

BURBAGE: (*interrupting*) I know that woman, who am I playing? Am I the Moor? Or am I King Richard?

TOOLEY: You are the Apothecary.

BURBAGE: The Apothecary? I don't recall a play about an Apothecary. Aha, Master Shakespeare has written me a new one!

HEMINGES: Nay...

TOOLEY: (*interrupting*) Aye, Master Shakespeare has written us a new play, 'The Apothecary of Mantua'.

BURBAGE: Am I a wealthy man?

TOOLEY: You are a great man of business, who visits the city of Verona.

BURBAGE: Ah, Verona, and I have an adventure there?

TOOLEY: Aye, a young man is coming to ask you for a draught of poison.

BURBAGE: Aha, there's always a draught of poison in an adventure, but I won't give it over without some money from the lad.

TOOLEY: Good, Master Burbage, you know your part.

CONDELL returns.

CONDELL: There is time, they will wait for him.

HEMINGES: (*aside*) Can a knock to the head restore so much to an old man?

TOOLEY: (*aside*) He might have been like this for years, and you would not have known it, for he's just been taking his cues from the rest of you.

HEMINGES: You think we did not notice a completely addled man, living amongst us?

TOOLEY: Living and working, cheek by jowl with you all, and you fools had no inkling. Get out of his costume.

CONDELL: I confess I did not see it. He's a clever old bird.

TOOLEY: I lived with many such people in the nunnery. Sometimes they need words more than they need food, but just a little goes a very long way. (*Coming to BURBAGE'S side*) Master Burbage, the Apothecary is on soon. You only need your cloak and hat.

> *HEMINGES removes the hat and cloak and hands them to TOOLEY, who makes a great show of putting the hat on, as though it was a crown.*

TOOLEY: (*cont'd*) You are the greatest Apothecary in Italy.

BURBAGE: Aye, and the whole story hinges on what potion I give to the hero.

TOOLEY: The noble Apothecary.

BURBAGE: What if they see that I am not what I say I am?

TOOLEY: When did Master Burbage become such a mewling kitten?

> *TOOLEY helps BURBAGE to stand and puts the cloak on him.*

BURBAGE: But if I forget?

TOOLEY: You forget, and if Richard Burbage forgets, he sits, and he is Burbage, and they watch, and they listen, and he finds his way back, and then he remembers. You are Richard Burbage, player of the Lord Chamberlain's Men.

BURBAGE: I am Richard Burbage, player.

> *TOOLEY checks on the progress of the play by peering onto the Globe stage.*

TOOLEY: Come, it is time.

> *TOOLEY helps BURBAGE up the steps. HEMINGES and CONDELL position themselves to watch what happens on the Globe stage.*

ACT TWO

HEMINGES: I still owe you that crown. Give me a chance to win it back?

CONDELL: You can have every coin on me, if Burbage fails.

HEMINGES: Done. Here he comes...

Both men are totally absorbed by what they are looking at. First they are silent, then HEMINGES smiles broadly as though BURBAGE'S failure is obvious.

CONDELL: Nay, don't start crowing yet, he has picked it up again.

HEMINGES: Taylor's ogling him, he must be on the wrong words.

CONDELL: It doesn't matter, he's leading them somewhere.

HEMINGES: He's going off the stage.

CONDELL: Tooley's probably feeding him a line, here he comes, back on, then right down to the people...

They both fall silent, floored by BURBAGE'S command of the audience. There is generous applause. HEMINGES throws a handful of coins at CONDELL'S feet and as they leave the steps, CONDELL collects the coins and HEMINGES sits. Unnoticed, TOOLEY returns halfway down the steps, stops, and listens to every word.

CONDELL: *(cont'd)* Are you sure that's all you've got?

HEMINGES turns out his pockets, all that falls out are torn scraps of play script.

CONDELL: *(laughing)* You have forgotten what it is to play. No player ever knows what will come out of his mouth when he walks onto the stage, you know that. If Burbage reads only half his lines, he makes up the other half of the illusion with all his hot air! Oh, I am filled with delight at the idea. We could go on playing until we're worse than Burbage is now, you and I.

HEMINGES: I may have to, Condell, I'll never *(cont'd)*

HEMINGES: (*cont'd*) play a new part, not now. I don't have Burbage's courage. What use is an old player who cannot read his lines?

CONDELL: We'll con your lines together, you and I. We don't have to tell anyone upstairs.

HEMINGES: Will you stand by my side when I am so blind I am about to fall off the stage, and cannot find my own way off?

CONDELL: We can count the number of paces from the back of the stage to the front.

HEMINGES: Every day I see less.

CONDELL: I know it, the work you did on Burbage's face was not always the best lately.

HEMINGES: I wanted a book of Will's plays. All the university fellows would have been happy to pay for it. I wanted to hold that in my hand, and retire, without any of the younger men knowing about my eyes.

CONDELL: You should have told us you were thinking about your book again, instead of just landing it on us.

HEMINGES: I wanted us to have enough coin to stay warm by our fires instead of playing until we go like Burbage.

CONDELL: (*Clowning*) Steady on, we're not as bad as Burbage, unless there's something you're not telling me? You'd tell me if I was, wouldn't you?

HEMINGES: If I could just see the words, I could do the whole thing myself, but even by the light of day my eyes are failing me.

CONDELL: Come now... how many plays did Will Shakespeare write?

HEMINGES: More than thirty.

CONDELL: Perchance almost forty. We'll just (*cont'd*)

ACT TWO

CONDELL: *(cont'd)* have to remember the bits that are missing, and write them down.

HEMINGES: We are all heading for our graves Condell, we don't have enough time to remember.

CONDELL: Nay, remembering roles is nothing. You won't need your eyes to remember any of yours. What we have in our heads was graven into our skulls. All of it, drilled every night so that any play might be called the next day. I barely remember my prayers, Heminges, but I remember every one of my lines! Did you not start out playing the hero's best friends? Then they moved you up to the gallant nobles and lords, long before you started doing the idle and fussy fathers?

HEMINGES: Aye, that's about the sum of it.

CONDELL: They started me on the hero's second-best friends, then I went to the clowns, and the sophisticated Fools, and I always did the gravediggers, even when I was young. Burbage did all the heroes, of course. Hamlet, Othello, Richard, Lear, and Tooley did all the wives and maidens. Between us, we are the complete plays of Master Shakespeare!

HEMINGES: Except Burbage has nothing in his receptacle.

HEMINGES sits in defeat, and CONDELL approaches him, awkwardly offering comfort. The crowd chants "Bur-bage, Bur-bage, Bur-bage!".

CONDELL: Then we'll sit down together and start from the beginning, like boys at school.

HEMINGES: Nay, Condell, you cannot clown me into it.

CONDELL: It's the job of a Fool to make men laugh, when all they want to do is cry.

More chanting: "Bur-bage, Bur-bage, Bur-bage!".

CONDELL: (*cont'd*) He'll be drinking up the admiration.

HEMINGES: Aye, he never forgets to go for another call, have you noticed!

TOOLEY: (*announcing his presence*) It is more than admiration. It is love.

HEMINGES: How long have you been standing there?

TOOLEY: (*to CONDELL*) You forgot about the queens.

CONDELL: The queens?

TOOLEY: I also played all the queens.

CONDELL: Aye, that's true enough.

HEMINGES: Tooley, forget what you think you heard.

TOOLEY: Burbage is coming, just make as though it's the old days. We are the Lord Chamberlain's Men now, remember?

CONDELL: Would that I cut the figure I did in the old days.

TOOLEY: Suck it in, just like the rest of us! Elizabeth sits on the throne, and Lear is not yet written.

HEMINGES: If it really is the old days, we are running the playhouse, then it's the complete fantasy...

TOOLEY: Just play it, and I'll try to draw him back to us from there.

As TOOLEY goes to ascend the stairs, BURBAGE stumbles his way down them.

BURBAGE: Out of the way woman!

BURBAGE hands his cape to TOOLEY and makes straight for the privy.

BURBAGE: (*while pissing*) Good crowd, again.

TOOLEY: You had them in your hands today.

TOOLEY encourages HEMINGES and CONDELL to make a show of support.

CONDELL: Fine work, Burbage.

HEMINGES: Aye, very fine.

BURBAGE: The crowd knows a good play when (*cont'd*)

ACT TWO

BURBAGE: (*cont'd*) it's shown one.

TOOLEY: But it was you they loved the most.

BURBAGE: I never seem to piss out as much as it feels I should...

BURBAGE finishes off and emerges.

BURBAGE: (*to TOOLEY*) I need a drink.

TOOLEY: Aye, Master Burbage.

BURBAGE: Pour one for all the men.

CONDELL rummages for cups and pours drinks from the barrel for all.

BURBAGE: (*cont'd*) Don't give drinks to the washer woman, it will only look bad for her.

TOOLEY indicates to CONDELL that he should obey.

BURBAGE: (*toasting*) To tomorrow's plays.

CONDELL/HEMINGES: Tomorrow's plays.

BURBAGE: (*to CONDELL and HEMINGES*) Leave me now.

BURBAGE downs his drink. TOOLEY encourages CONDELL and HEMINGES to withdraw up the stairs.

TOOLEY: (*aside*) You tried getting the words out of Burbage your way, Heminges. Both of you, leave us, and let me try mine.

CONDELL refills his cup and he and HEMINGES reluctantly ascend the steps. TOOLEY gathers costumes, checking that they have really gone.

BURBAGE: Woman, have they said what plays we're doing tomorrow?

TOOLEY: Nay, Master Burbage.

BURBAGE: Go and ask Master Shakespeare, and I'll give you a coin, lass.

TOOLEY: Aye.

TOOLEY retreats halfway up the steps. BURBAGE waits until he is sure he is alone, then opens his box with the key from around his neck. From inside, he draws out (cont'd) (cont'd) various small books – quarto play editions – laying them out carefully, as though going through the contents of his brain, reading bits and pieces, laughing at some, quoting others, trying various moves. TOOLEY makes a noise on purpose, then returns. BURBAGE throws a piece of clothing over the open box and the laid-out papers.

TOOLEY: *(cont'd)* Dickie, come, it is time to prepare for tomorrow's plays.

BURBAGE: Is there anyone about?

TOOLEY: Nay, they're all upstairs counting the money.

BURBAGE tries to grab TOOLEY into an embrace.

BURBAGE: Give us a kiss first.

TOOLEY: *(dodging)* Nay, Master Shakespeare said we'll be starting with one of our old favourites. Can you guess?

BURBAGE: The one about the plucky little legal lass?

TOOLEY: Nay, more favoured than Portia.

BURBAGE: More favoured than Portia? I liked her well enough. Who did I like better than her?

TOOLEY: "Deny thy father and refuse thy name; Or, if thou wilt not, be but sworn my love, and I'll no longer be a Capulet."

BURBAGE: Juliet!

TOOLEY: Aye. Come, we'll run your lines from the death scene.

TOOLEY pulls a prop hamper into the centre.

TOOLEY: *(cont'd)* You, Romeo, enter the chapel of the Capulets, and, I, Juliet, am lying here.

BURBAGE: Dead.

TOOLEY: Nay, I am not dead, I only sleep, but to you, it is as though I am dead.

TOOLEY: "Ah, dear Juliet, why art thou yet so fair?"

Seeming confident, BURBAGE takes over the lines seamlessly and comes to TOOLEY'S side.

ACT TWO

BURBAGE/ROMEO: "Shall I believe that unsubstantial death is amorous, and that..." (*he dries*). Don't tell me, I know it. "Shall I believe that unsubstantial death is amorous, and that..." (*he dries*).

BURBAGE goes to his box and papers.

TOOLEY: Dickie?

BURBAGE: Wait! Stay there Juliet, you sleep!

BURBAGE goes to his box and papers. HEMINGES and CONDELL reappear on the steps, creeping silently into a position where they can see and hear everything happening between BURBAGE and TOOLEY.

BURBAGE: (*cont'd*) "Ay me, sweet Juliet, are thy still so fair? Do I believe that death loves thee too much..."

TOOLEY opens her eyes and sees the quarto script in BURBAGE'S hand, gently takes it and throws it away.

TOOLEY: You do not need this printer's rubbish, Dickie. Let it go.

BURBAGE: I knew the lines once, I knew them all...

TOOLEY tenderly places a hand on BURBAGE'S face.

TOOLEY: We still know them all, my love.

TOOLEY starts to speak Romeo's lines, encouraging BURBAGE to speak them too.

TOOLEY/ROMEO: "Ah, dear Juliet, why art thou yet so fair? Shall I believe that unsubstantial death is amorous, and that the lean abhorred monster keeps thee here in dark to be his paramour?"

TOOLEY continues to say the lines, but gradually she plays dead, resting her head against BURBAGE'S shoulder, feeding the lines into his ear. It creates a mesmerising illusion that BURBAGE still knows all his lines.

TOOLEY/BURBAGE/ROMEO: "For fear of that, I still will stay with thee; and never from this palace of dim night depart again: here, here will I remain with worms that are thy chamber-maids; O, here (*cont'd*)

TOOLEY/BURBAGE/ROMEO: *(cont'd)* will I set up my everlasting rest, and shake the yoke of inauspicious stars from this world-wearied flesh. Eyes, look your last! Arms, take your last embrace! And, lips, O you the doors of breath, seal with a righteous kiss. A dateless bargain to engrossing death!"

They kiss, passionately.

BURBAGE: You know my lines better than I do, woman.

TOOLEY: The last time we did that was before the Queen. I could see her from my tomb, for her dress it was all dandied-up with little jewels, and in the light of the candles they did flicker. But in the darkness where her face should be, two watery jewels hung for her eyes, and I knew then that good Queen Bess had known love the way Juliet had known it, the way I had known it, at least once before she went to her grave, God rest her soul.

BURBAGE: Good Queen Bess, she is gone to her grave?

TOOLEY: Oh... nay, Dickie.

BURBAGE: Do they laugh when it's a comedy, or do they laugh when it's a tragedy?

TOOLEY: Come, more of *Romeo and Juliet*, sit by me.

BURBAGE: My Juliet promised she would always be there, when I came off the stage, but she lied.

TOOLEY: Perchance she had to go?

BURBAGE: I never released her.

TOOLEY: But you did not come after her. She was past the age of an apprentice, well past. There was nothing more for her to play, and she could not stay and play your wife any longer.

BURBAGE: It was she who sent me to the printers.

TOOLEY: She? How?

BURBAGE drops the box and papers.

ACT TWO

BURBAGE: I didn't need any of this until she left. I heard it said, you see, that a printer would be a very good friend to an old player. The printers said they could put all my words together in one place, on these cunning little pages (*he holds up a quarto*) where they could never be forgotten. King Richard I gave to printer Thomas Creede. Thomas Pavier, he took King Lear off my mind, and Richard Smethwick, he got my prizes... Hamlet and Romeo. But they lied to me too. Always cutting, always changing... they were never word-perfect.

TOOLEY: Rest now Dickie.

BURBAGE: I think she is gone, our Queen, and I think we are not playing this play tomorrow. I told Mrs Burbage I would be home tonight. I must take all these papers home to keep her warm.

> HEMINGES *moves straight for* BURBAGE'S *box.* CONDELL *follows.*

HEMINGES: How much did the printers pay you, Burbage?

> *The shock of their discovery strikes* BURBAGE *into a frail state and* TOOLEY *into ashamed silence.*

BURBAGE: "Romeo! Romeo! Wherefore are thou roaming now? Tell thy father and give up thy name; Or alone alas I will remain."

HEMINGES: Why didn't you just give Will's copies to the printers?

BURBAGE: Will's copies? They were never Will's copies! A playwright never owns the copies, he only writes a play down, in handwriting no player could ever read, and he sells his foul scribblings to the playhouse. When a player has conned his lines, he can do whatever he likes with the papers.

HEMINGES: When we are gone, where is the (*cont'd*)

HEMINGES: (*cont'd*) play then? It will not hang in the air of a playhouse, it cannot be drawn down by another player.

BURBAGE: When we are gone, so too will the plays be gone. That is the way it has been since long before we walked the stage, and that is the way it will be long after we are all in our graves.

HEMINGES: Burbage...

BURBAGE: Silence! No player will ever own my parts. He might play Romeo right now, that leggy player, but it is my part, mine! He is only borrowing it. He is only parroting me.

HEMINGES: But what of Master Shakespeare?

BURBAGE: When we are gone, none will have further need of him.

> *BURBAGE brushes a hand gently across TOOLEY'S cheek, and ascends the stairs.*

HEMINGES: How many of Burbage's parts do you know?

TOOLEY: All. We drilled them enough.

HEMINGES: Every one?

TOOLEY: You know the job of an apprentice as well as I: copy the lines for your Master, from the playwright's pages, and cue him when he forgets.

CONDELL: Aye, we all of us did it, but to have remembered all of Burbage's, and all your own, that is the task of a lifetime.

TOOLEY: There were too many lines for one man to hold by himself, so I just kept up the remembering.

HEMINGES: Why did you not say so before?

TOOLEY: Because it would have shown Master Burbage up. Sometimes it is wiser to make believe, for the sake of another man. It's something you could have tried long ago, Heminges.

ACT TWO

HEMINGES goes through BURBAGE'S locked box.

HEMINGES: Every printed play is here, but none of it is as Shakespeare wrote it. Quickly, gather Will's copies together, and we'll put them back together. I'll take it all to the Stationers', now, before the printer's boys are finished their scribbling.

HEMINGES starts to collate Shakespeare's copies. TOOLEY retires to her stool and starts packing away her things. CONDELL notices.

CONDELL: I can see it now, this book.

HEMINGES: Oh, it'll be bigger than a book, more like a folio.

CONDELL: A folio?

HEMINGES: It would be wise to set the price at a neat pound.

CONDELL: A bargain, considering the cost.

HEMINGES: Oh, by the time they've set the type and paid for all the inks, there won't be too much change from a pound.

CONDELL: Aye, the material costs will be great.

HEMINGES: Well, what other costs will there be?

CONDELL: Oh, I think there is a cost, if you think about it.

HEMINGES: Think about what?

CONDELL: Make sure you have all the words first, especially the missing ones.

CONDELL indicates that HEMINGES needs to address TOOLEY. HEMINGES looks frustrated, then compliant, puts the copies down and goes TOOLEY'S side.

HEMINGES: Where are you going, Master Tooley? There is our curtain call yet, and you've earned it! Where are we up to?

TOOLEY: *(checks on the stage)* I missed the death scene... there is not much left to play now. How easily *(cont'd)*

MERELY PLAYERS

TOOLEY: *(cont'd)* I slipped back into my old place in this playhouse, right at the bottom of the heap. The fetcher, the one who picks the clothes up off the floor, and reminds all of you where the play is up to.

CONDELL: What you have, in your receptacle, it belongs to the King's Men, to all of us, and therefore so do you.

TOOLEY: It has been a very long time since I have belonged anywhere.

HEMINGES: Give us the words. It will not go unrewarded.

TOOLEY: Men like me, we are just a spectacle for the freak shows.

HEMINGES: Listen, these printed plays, they print players' names on them, do they not? We could add all our names to this folio. A man who has his name on a book of Shakespeare's plays could never be thought of as a freak-show spectacle.

CONDELL: Shakespeare should go at the top of the page.

HEMINGES: Then Burbage.

CONDELL: Then you, Heminges.

HEMINGES: Only if such a position is warranted.

CONDELL: Of course it is warranted.

HEMINGES: Well, you should go next.

CONDELL: Nay, I would not go on the list above my Master's name. All the masters must go first.

HEMINGES: Alright, that's Phillips, and Pope, and Master Kempe. Then you, surely, at the top of the younger clowns.

CONDELL: Only if you think I should go there.

HEMINGES: Then the younger heroes. They'd best go in or they'll take it badly and run off to another playhouse.

ACT TWO

CONDELL: Put Lowin, and Cooke... but what of old Master Armin? Put him up there somewhere.

HEMINGES: Aye, if they're gone to their graves, and were shareholders, they must have a good position. We'll have to make a proper account of all the men, but tomorrow.

TOOLEY: What of all the women?

HEMINGES: What?

TOOLEY: You haven't mentioned anyone who played a woman.

HEMINGES: Well, how many more words will that be?

TOOLEY: Oh, I have so many words in my head that a printer would have to sell his house to ink them, Master Heminges, but I would give them all, for only two words from you in return.

HEMINGES: Two? Which two?

TOOLEY: You can put my name on your book. I can do without Master Tooley now. I haven't needed him for many years. You can have him.

HEMINGES: We might need to have two lists on the page, one on the left and one on the right.

CONDELL: Who goes at the top of the right-hand side?

HEMINGES: That could flow on from the bottom of the left-hand side.

CONDELL: But if a player's name goes top right, but he's not a top player, we'll get complaints.

HEMINGES: I can see no other way to do it.

TOOLEY: Have some of the King's Men done more than others?

HEMINGES: It could be a matter of the number of parts played.

TOOLEY: Master Shakespeare played but a few parts, and he's at the top of this list of yours. It seems to me you're putting all the skirt players at the *(cont'd)*

TOOLEY: *(cont'd)* bottom of the list, or nowhere.

HEMINGES: Some of them were on the stage so little, just a queen here or a maiden there. We cannot give the same place to boys as we give to men.

TOOLEY: We boys have long since grown into men, while your men have grown into dust. Remember all of us, or none.

HEMINGES: I can see we are going to have to think on this, another time. I must get Will's copies to the Stationer. Where are we up to?

TOOLEY: Let you not think on it too long, Master Heminges. If you want me to give you the contents of my receptacle, you'd best get in fast.

HEMINGES: I can see you would keep your secrets.

TOOLEY: It is up to you, Master Heminges.

HEMINGES: Just like a woman! Always it is up to a man to work out the ways of a woman! Would that you thought on this as a man would!

TOOLEY: It was a woman who got the words for you.

HEMINGES: Which woman?

TOOLEY: It was Juliet who raised Romeo for you, right before your eyes.

HEMINGES: And I suppose you and Burbage... it wasn't all an act, duckie?

CONDELL: I think we can guess the answer, Heminges.

TOOLEY: He rewarded me in ways that I needed, in ways that he found he needed.

HEMINGES: Can your base needs have been anything like love?

TOOLEY: "O, reason not the need! Our basest beggars are in the poorest thing superfluous. Allow not nature more than nature needs, man's life's as cheap as beast's."

HEMINGES: Quote me no more of Will's words, *(cont'd)*

ACT TWO

HEMINGES: (*cont'd*) Tooley...

TOOLEY: "But, for true need, you heavens, give me that patience, patience I need. You see me here, you gods, a poor old man, as full of grief as age, wretched in both."

HEMINGES: You can turn the words whichever way you like, it won't ever make them true.

TOOLEY: If you print the words, people will make more use of them than you can imagine.

HEMINGES: I could report you for sodomy, if you do not want to share what it is that you hold.

TOOLEY: I would rather die a happy sodomite than an unhappy player.

HEMINGES: You are very good with words, Master Tooley.

TOOLEY: Women like me must wield words the way men like you wield swords.

HEMINGES: You think you're the only man here who needs? Look at us, Condell and me. His face is so thick with paint because he thinks it means the young clowns will have another year behind him. He has eight families to feed with his shares. I have more, and soon I will not be able to see the roles to con them into my receptacle, and they will find a way to get me out of this playhouse, unless you give me those words and you come with us in this printing plan.

TOOLEY: How bad are your eyes?

HEMINGES: Sometimes I confuse the names of the little ones playing at my feet. They laugh at me, but soon I will be confusing everyone else, and I won't be able to hide it.

TOOLEY: I've already said you can have the words.

HEMINGES: And I've already said you can have your name on the book.

CONDELL: Then you both need the other, that has been clear from the minute Master Tooley returned.

TOOLEY: You don't even know my name. I had to leave the convent because they found out I was not a real woman, so I wrote to Mrs Burbage, to see if Burbage would take me back, but it was not as Nicholas Tooley.

CONDELL: There, I am right. Master Tooley... or whatever your name is, need not fear, the King's Men will not put him... her, out on the street. We'll put... her, to work in the playhouse.

TOOLEY: I confess there is another reason. When I went to remember my lines, I did not have them so well as I used.

CONDELL: It has been ten years.

TOOLEY: Nay, it is more than time. If I wait too long, I fear my words will go like Burbage's.

CONDELL: A brave confession for a player. And you, Heminges?

HEMINGES: What?

CONDELL: What do you confess?

HEMINGES: I, confess? I confess that when the sun rose this day, that I never saw it would set with things the way they are.

CONDELL: And... what else?

HEMINGES: What else? I confess I never thought there would come a day when a man in a skirt would hold so much in his hands as he does, right now, before us...

CONDELL: And... cough it up, Heminges.

HEMINGES: And that man would ask so little in return.

CONDELL: Man? All I see here is you, and me, and one fine lady of the stage.

HEMINGES: I cannot make believe Tooley is a *(cont'd)*

ACT TWO

HEMINGES: *(cont'd)* real woman off the stage. What if one of the other men notices me calling him by a woman's name?

CONDELL: You could just pretend it's your bad eyes.

HEMINGES: I don't think I have it in me.

CONDELL: Oh, it won't take much, just two little words.

HEMINGES: Which two?

TOOLEY crosses to HEMINGES, curtsies and puts her hand out to be kissed.

TOOLEY: Mistress Wilkinson, very pleased to make your acquaintance, Master Heminges.

HEMINGES seems unwilling.

TOOLEY: *(cont'd)* It's half right. Have you forgotten? Master Shakespeare called me that when he picked me for Juliet.

HEMINGES: Wilkinson?

TOOLEY: Aye. I was just thirteen, and he did not want my mama to pluck me off the stage if the Puritans found out Juliet was a boy by the name of Tooley. The Burbage women have always been happy to call me Mistress Wilkinson, in public.

HEMINGES: And Mrs Burbage knows nothing, about you and her husband?

TOOLEY: Oh, I think she has always suspected, but she has said nothing. She only wants someone to stay close to Dickie, to get him home. That is enough for me. If there's something to play, I can do it. It will suit me better than trying to fool the priests.

CONDELL: There's a man.

HEMINGES goes as if to shake TOOLEY'S hand.

HEMINGES: There's a King's Man.

TOOLEY turns over his hand.

TOOLEY: Here's nothing but a player.

And HEMINGES kisses it.

CONDELL: *(back to business)* We will ink every man's name after Shakespeare and Burbage, in the order that he came into his shares, whether he lives or has gone to his grave.

TOOLEY: That's fair. You can ink Nicholas Tooley as though he were dead.

CONDELL: Just one page, so it won't add much to the cost.

HEMINGES: Agreed. Now, help me with the pages, there is no time to do more than bundle them together.

CONDELL: Aye.

TOOLEY: I'll help you search after I've done what I've been needing to do since I came off.

TOOLEY goes to the privy and shuts the curtain. CONDELL and HEMINGES retrieve scraps of paper from throughout the room, flattening and sorting them.

HEMINGES: We'll have to play the poet, you and I.

CONDELL: How so?

HEMINGES: We'll have to fill in the gaps, and there'll be plenty. Not just with dross, with poetry as good as Will Shakespeare's.

CONDELL: Well, as long as you don't play the pedant too often.

HEMINGES: What do you mean?

CONDELL: "Write down the page, put every character's name in a large hand, so it can be seen. Are you putting in the gestures and moves?"

HEMINGES: I never said that.

CONDELL: Did.

HEMINGES: I would never say "moves", I'd say "enter" and "exit".

CONDELL: That's better.

ACT TWO

HEMINGES: Now you're sounding just like a printer.

TOOLEY emerges from the privy with a stack of papers.

TOOLEY: Here's more play.

CONDELL: What, just sitting in the privy?

TOOLEY: Aye, the privy paper... there is plenty.

TOOLEY returns to the privy, and, with one hand pinching her nose, returns with the pot, takes the covering off, and points into it.

HEMINGES: There's more, in there?

TOOLEY nods.

HEMINGES: (*to CONDELL*) You'll have to read it, I can't see a thing, remember?

CONDELL: (*to TOOLEY*) We'll both do it. Hold it steady. (*He holds his nose and gets closer*) "Is love a tender thing? It is too rough, too rude, too boisterous, and it pricks like thorn..."

HEMINGES/MERCUTIO: "If love be rough with you, be rough with love; Prick love for pricking, and you beat love down." That's Mercutio.

CONDELL: *Romeo and Juliet*.

HEMINGES: How much of it?

TOOLEY: (*reading the privy paper pile*) Looks like most of it, apart from what's been used already on every man's pissy fingers, and we could piece those together.

TOOLEY hands HEMINGES the chamber pot and collates the rest.

CONDELL: If you leave now, you can still beat the printer's boys to the Stationer!

HEMINGES: Montague is supposed to be on, in the last scene.

CONDELL: What say I add a new jig to the end of *Romeo and Juliet*, fifteen verses, with plenty of new words in a complicated double-rhyme, which the printer's boys won't want to miss a single word (*cont'd*)

CONDELL: (*cont'd*) of. Will that give you a head start?

HEMINGES: I could be on the other side of the river by the time you bring it down.

TOOLEY: (*peering onto the Globe stage*) There is no need. Burbage is on.

HEMINGES, CONDELL and TOOLEY all look onto the Globe stage.

HEMINGES: What's he doing?

TOOLEY: He's padding it out.

HEMINGES: What's he playing?

TOOLEY: Bits of *Hamlet*, by the sounds. The printer's boys are looking at one another.

CONDELL: He knows what he's doing, the old devil.

TOOLEY: Now he's starting on bits of *Macbeth*.

HEMINGES: How did he know we needed time?

TOOLEY: An addled man still has ears and eyes. You might ask him for help in the morning, and he'll deliver it, but not till the afternoon. (*Handing pages to HEMINGES*) There is enough of *Romeo and Juliet* here for you to say it is complete.

HEMINGES: (*holding up the chamber pot*) What about the bits in here?

TOOLEY: Well... (*shrugging*) that's the rest of it.

CONDELL: The stationers cannot complain what form the words are in, now can they?

TOOLEY: Nay, it's never word-perfect.

CONDELL: Take it, go. We'll follow with the rest.

HEMINGES: We're taking all the plays to the Stationers' Guild, tonight?

CONDELL: Why not?

HEMINGES: All these bloodied and pissy papers, matched with our failing memories... now that we have agreed to it I scarcely see how it can be done. It will take us years to make a book of all Will (*cont'd*)

ACT TWO

HEMINGES: *(cont'd)* Shakespeare's plays.

CONDELL: Years of making trouble, and it's bound to get us back upstairs, you said so yourself. Come, Tooley, we'll need to use Burbage's box to carry it all. When the printers are done with all this it will certainly be ready for Mrs Burbage's fire.

TOOLEY: I'll get out of my women's weeds first.

HEMINGES: Nay, come as you are, it matters not.

CONDELL: Are you still here? Go!

HEMINGES exits up the steps with papers under his arm, bearing the chamber pot.

CONDELL: *(cont'd)* I don't know about you, but I say Shakespeare's *Romeo and Juliet* stinks!

TOOLEY: Aye, you could say every one of us left our mark on it.

CONDELL: *(peering onto the Globe stage)* Look at Burbage, he has the crowd right in his hands. You could almost believe he played us all, getting you back, letting us argue about shares, and waiting, until Master Heminges' printing plan was back on the table.

TOOLEY: "All the world's a stage, and all the men and women..."

CONDELL/TOOLEY: "...merely players."

CONDELL: That's my line... well, it was my line.

TOOLEY: We should go. I'll help you to the river. I want to be here when he comes off.

CONDELL and TOOLEY gather all the copies and exit with them up the steps, as the dressing room disappears from view, revealing BURBAGE on the stage.

BURBAGE/MACBETH: "Tomorrow, and tomorrow, and tomorrow,
Creeps in this petty pace from day to day
To the last syllable of recorded time,
And all our yesterdays have lighted fools *(cont'd)*

BURBAGE/MACBETH: (*cont'd*) The way to dusty death..." (*he dries*).
"Out, out, brief candle!
Life's but a walking shadow, a poor player
That struts and frets his hour upon the stage
And then is heard no more. It is a tale
Told by an idiot, full of sound and fury,
Signifying nothing." (*Fade*).

Shakespeare

A farmer who cultivated words

NO WRITER IN the English language ever had their life and times examined as much as William Shakespeare, a native of the rural Warwickshire market town of Stratford-upon-Avon, who went on to become the world's greatest playwright.

With few known facts and little primary evidence, speculation by academics, impresarios, directors and eccentrics has created the various 'lives' of Shakespeare that so often go unquestioned.

Just as many theories discredit Shakespeare, painting him as an uneducated buffoon from a farming backwater who must have covered for an educated person more deserving of the title 'the greatest English playwright'.

But there is one easily overlooked element to Shakespeare's work which indelibly links him – and his plays – to Warwickshire: his use of that county's unique vernacular throughout his work.

Much of the Warwickshire jargon in Shakespeare is the vocabulary that anyone who grew up in the parish of Stratford would have picked up from a very young age, and needed little formal education in.

Long before writing plays for the realm's premier theatre company at London's Globe playhouse, William Shakespeare was born into a family like most in Warwickshire – one with strong farming connections, and rural language.

Shakespeare's Father, John, was at various times a leatherworker and glovemaker, and a wool dealer who served as an alderman on the local council. His mother Mary Arden's family farmed for centuries in the Stratford region.

Although by the time Shakespeare was born his family were 'townies' living on Henley Street in Stratford-upon-Avon, both sets of his grandparents were farmers.

The Shakespeares had been tenant farmers on land owned by the Ardens, but there is plenty of evidence Shakespeare's father broadened the family interests away from the graft of running farms to a more genteel, lucrative and often illegal income as a landowner, agricultural trader and money-lender.

And although he went on to achieve literary fame, his son William also followed his father's rural buying and selling footsteps for his entire life.

If Shakespeare picked up an early education on the rural landscape from an array of older family members, by the time he was a trader in his own right, the language of cropping and grain selling, animal husbandry and wool sales, and the production of food and clothing from grain, fibre and hide, well and truly completed his knowledge of all things farming.

That's not to say he poured this experience into his popular entertainments. Rather, like inconvenient seedlings throughout his work, they 'crop up'.

It was historian Michael Wood who underlined Shakespeare's use of the term 'hayd land' in *Henry IV Part 2* in his series *In Search of Shakespeare*. Referring to a strip of land left uncultivated when a Warwickshire ploughman turned his plough around, London typesetters unfamiliar with the original term inserted it as 'hade land' in printed versions of the play.

Like Wood, Scott McCrea, in his book *The Case for Shakespeare: The End of the Authorship Question*, identified another piece of rural slang: "In *Antony and Cleopatra*, Scarus's simile of 'the breeze upon her, like a cow in June' makes little sense until it's understood that breeze means stinging gadfly in Warwickshire."

Other researchers see reflections of a significant rural event – The Midland Revolt – in Shakespeare's Roman tragedy *Coriolanus*. The infamous 1607 uprising saw thousands protest from Northamptonshire to Warwickshire and Leicestershire, unhappy at the latest round of Enclosure Acts that locked farmland away from common use.

The grain shortages in *Coriolanus* have parallels with the revolt, although any of the alternative authors suggested for Shakespeare's plays – such as Cambridge graduate Christopher Marlowe – could have strung the contemporary reports of the Midland Revolt into a play; whereas if you really seek to claim Marlowe wrote Shakespeare's plays, you're going to have to prove the Kent-born dramatist knew a swathe of Warwickshire slang; and not just workaday words easily picked up in any market square, but practical farmers' trading terms, the kind that typesetters got wrong in the 17th century and citified actors misinterpret to the present day.

You'll also need to show how a great writer of tragedies like Marlowe was savvy enough to use these words to comic effect.

Shakespeare didn't require any special education to include the discussion on the price of sheep in *Henry IV Part 2* between his comic characters Silence and Shallow. Nor did he have any problem accurately portraying the correct price of wool when a shepherd in *The Winter's Tale* attempts to calculate the value of his fleeces:

"Let me see: every 'leven wether tods; every tod yields pound and odd shilling; fifteen hundred shorn. What comes the wool to?"

One of the earliest eyewitness accounts of Shakespeare's dual literary–farming legacy in Stratford-upon-Avon came in 1708, when London actor and theatre manager Thomas Betterton visited.

Almost a century after the town's most famous son had died, there was no sign of the tourist mecca that Stratford-upon-Avon would become. For a chunk of the interim period, including the Civil War, plays had been considered sinful and anyone who had anything to do with them treated as scum.

Betterton recounted what he found to dramatist, poet and Shakespeare editor Nicholas Rowe, who used it to write the first biography of the Stratford Shakespeares in 1709 – the basis for much of the later research on the subject of William Shakespeare.

Whether it was a case of Betterton's bad memory, or an oversight by engraver Gerard Van der Gucht, there was no quill or parchment in the engraving in Rowe's book of the only visible remnant of William Shakespeare in Stratford-upon-Avon in 1709 – the monument and bust of the playwright in the town's Holy Trinity Church.

Instead, there is what appears to be either a bag of grain, or a wool bale.

This yawning gap between a man who wrote plays and poems, many of which became pre-eminent in the English language, who never went to university and cannot be proven to have attended school – yet also made a significant living as a land and agricultural commodities trader – has always been too great for many in the British establishment.

By 1725, when another image of the Shakespeare bust appeared, someone had added a quill and parchment to the monument. Those who seek to separate Shakespeare the playwright from Shakespeare the farmer use this mysterious action as evidence that he did not write the plays that forever made his name.

I have something in common with William Shakespeare. I hale from a small farming community and, after we moved off the land, I went on to become a writer. Apart from one year at university, where I started an Arts degree, my tertiary education consisted of vocational training in the performing arts, which was undoubtedly more than Shakespeare received.

Nobody knows for sure how Shakespeare got to London and took up acting and writing. There are missing years when he cannot be found trading in Warwickshire's farming records, but his name – or a version of it – appears in a terse review by playwright and Cambridge graduate Robert Greene, who attempted to put a young upstart in the London theatre scene of the 1590s in his place.

Alluding to a line in Shakespeare's *Henry IV Part 3*: "O tiger's heart wrapped in a woman's hide", Greene wrote:

"...for there is an upstart Crow, beautified with our feathers, that with his Tygers hart wrapt in a Players hyde, supposes he is as well able to bombast out a blanke verse as the best of you: and being an absolute Johannes fac totum, is in his owne conceit the onely Shake-scene in a countrey."

You have to hand it to Greene – his ticking-off of the young Shakespeare is witty. Not only does he call the younger dramatist a 'Jack of all trades', the use of

MERELY PLAYERS

'Shake-scene' cements exactly who this 'Jack' is.

Greene also shows off his knowledge of Latin, his audience being university graduates, whose 'feathers' he accuses Shakespeare of using to call himself a serious playwright, although it's hard to overlook the academic snobbery aimed at a non-graduate who had airs above his station.

When I lived, studied and worked in the United Kingdom, I encountered the same competitive spirit. A vocational education in theatre practice was never enough to get me work on a stage or a studio, whereas declaring my country roots landed me a job in rural media in a flash. I suspect what has been in place ever since Greene's put-down of Shakespeare is the pathway of entitlement that runs from Oxbridge straight to the West End.

Whenever British playwrights made a splash without a university education – the likes of Joe Orton, John Osborne and Tom Stoppard – there was a chorus from the establishment reminiscent of Robert Greene's begrudging comments.

But William Shakespeare is an inspiration to this former farm boy who also became a writer, because he will forever wear the crown over the likes of Greene, having employed nothing but his 'owne conceit'; and despite adding more than 1700 words to the English language, he also remembered those of his childhood landscape.

He remains an unsurpassed Jack of all trades who was a master yarn spinner, which, as anyone from the country will tell you, is exactly how they breed them in the bush.

Acknowledgements

MANY THANKS TO fellow writer and actor Patsy Trench for several reads of *Merely Players* over the years, and plenty of insightful feedback. I'm also indebted to writers Sarah Michell and Elizabeth Ferretti, and journalist Daniel Seed, for reading and proofreading this edition ahead of its publication and helping to unearth the title's final shape.

I'd also like to pay tribute to the actors who took part in readings of the play between 2008 and 2012, both paid and voluntary. To all those who started with my script and generously extended it, I am thankful.

Sources about Nicholas Tooley include: 'Yeomen, Citizens, Gentlemen, and Players: The Burbages and Their Connections' by Mary Edmond, from *Elizabethan Theater: Essays in Honor of S. Schoenbaum*, edited by Samuel Schoenbaum, R. B. Parker, Sheldon P. Zitner (1996). Edmond cites: *Simon Forman casebook* (Bodleian Library, Oxford); and *Playhouse wills, 1558–1642: an edition of wills by Shakespeare and his contemporaries in the London theatre*, edited by E. A. J. Honigmann and S. Brock (1993).

Other sources: 'Mary Frith at the Fortune' by Mark Hutchings, from *Early Theatre* (2007); and *Audition: Everything an Actor Needs to Know to Get the Part* by Michael Shurtleff (Walker, 1978).

'LGBTI Labour's Lost' was first published as 'The incredible, 400-year-old story of William Shakespeare's transgender actor' in *Gay Star News*.

'Shakespeare – a farmer who cultivated words' was first published in my eBook *Pluck: Exploits of the single-minded*.

www.ingramcontent.com/pod-product-compliance
Lightning Source LLC
Chambersburg PA
CBHW070603300426
44113CB00010B/1376